The Crypto Gender Gap

The Crypto Gender Gap

Women Shaping the New Economy

Jahan Vespari

Mindful Pages

Published in 2026

ISBN: 9789374596425 (PB)
ISBN: 9789374597651 (eBook)

Published by

Mindful Pages
Imprint of Alpha Editions LLC
312 W. 2nd St #1834
Casper, WY 82601, USA

Content

Introduction

The first boom was measured in charts that rose like fever lines, in late-night trades executed on phones glowing beneath duvets, in headlines that treated price as destiny and volatility as spectacle. What went largely unrecorded were the quieter rooms where the real work took place: cramped co-working spaces where women translated cryptographic abstractions into tools a market vendor in Accra or a gig worker in Manchester could actually use; modest online channels where designers fought for clarity in interfaces others dismissed as mere polish; community groups where organisers stitched together trust long before any protocol achieved scale. While speculative capital shouted, these builders carried on almost unheard. Their contribution remained essential yet peripheral, noted only when systems failed and someone asked who had kept the everyday machinery running.

This silence is more than an oversight. It reveals a paradox at the heart of crypto's first decade. A technology hailed for its promise to dissolve gatekeeping had a remarkable knack for reconstructing old hierarchies under new banners. Early rhetoric insisted that participation was open to all, yet the distribution of voice, reward, and recognition reproduced patterns familiar from earlier technological shifts: the visible work skewed male, the invisible labour—documentation, stewardship, user support—was carried largely by women and rarely counted as innovation. In this disconnect between story and structure lies the starting point of this book.

Consider a scene that has repeated itself from San Francisco to Singapore: a bustling meet-up in the early days of crypto, dominated by jargon-laden bravado, diagrams scribbled at speed, and fortunes predicted with the confidence of weather oracles. In the corner, a woman who had spent the previous week testing wallet recovery sequences with first-time users quietly pointed out that the product's design made catastrophic loss almost inevitable. Her observation was correct, later proven by incidents that could have been avoided, yet in that moment it floated past the room like background noise. Visionaries were celebrated for risk-taking; guardians of safety were treated as ancillary. The consequences of such selective listening shaped not only teams and products, but the culture of the field itself.

A historical echo sits beneath this narrative. Technology has long displayed a habit of amnesia, forgetting the contributions of those whose labour does not fit the myth of the lone genius. Women coded the early algorithms that guided space exploration, managed the first large computer systems, and built the usability foundations that made the internet accessible to millions. Yet their impact rarely shaped the dominant stories of progress. Crypto, despite its rhetoric of disruption, followed a similar script. Its early communities prized speed over reflection, experimentation over maintenance, showmanship over rigour. In such an environment, the individuals who emphasised clarity, governance, or long-term resilience often appeared as outsiders—until the moment their absence became painfully visible.

This book sets out to correct that imbalance, not by lamenting exclusions but by revealing the deeper truth: women have shaped the new crypto economy in ways more significant, enduring, and practical than the headlines ever acknowledged. Their vantage points broaden our understanding of what decentralisation can achieve when stripped of its mythology and grounded in real human needs. This is not a celebration of individuals for symbolic purposes. It is an exploration of the work—strategic, operational, cultural—that transforms a technology from an idea into a system people can trust with their livelihoods.

What follows is an inquiry grounded in evidence and informed by stories from founders, engineers, policy shapers, product designers, security specialists, community leaders, and organisers who turned abstract architectures into usable tools. They reveal the mechanisms that widen participation, the design choices that foster safety, the governance patterns that listen rather than dictate, and the economic models that support—not exploit—the communities they serve. Through their experiences, we gain a clearer lens on the questions that matter: Who gets to build? Who benefits? Who bears the hidden risks? And what structures allow innovation to become genuinely inclusive rather than cosmetically diverse?

The argument of this book rests on a simple but often overlooked observation. Every technology is shaped less by what it enables in theory than by who is empowered to define its norms. A supposedly open ecosystem can be exclusionary in practice if entry requires time, financial capital, or cultural fluency available only to a narrow slice of the population. Early crypto projects often rewarded those willing to stake large sums, spend weekends at hackathons, or navigate complex governance structures. These incentives filtered out caregivers, late joiners, people working multiple jobs, and anyone seeking predictable pathways rather than speculative bets. When participation becomes dependent on performative risk appetite, the resulting culture privileges bravado over deliberation. A system built on such foundations will inevitably struggle to serve those whose lives depend on stability rather than spectacle.

Yet, across countless communities, women quietly challenged these norms. They designed onboarding flows that reduced cognitive burden; they pushed for paid discovery programmes instead of unpaid sprints; they questioned token models that rewarded early insiders disproportionately; they tested resilience rather than chasing hype. Their approach was rarely celebrated as leadership, yet it demonstrated precisely the systems thinking that decentralised technology requires. Where others spoke about financial freedom, they built mechanisms that actually delivered it to households otherwise excluded from formal banking. Where others championed sovereignty, they created safeguards that made self-custody a responsibility rather than a trap. Theirs was a vision rooted in practicality: liberation through usability, empowerment through transparency, innovation through inclusion.

The more one studies these contributions, the more a pattern emerges—a motif that threads through every chapter of this book. Crypto's true potential lies not in its ability to eliminate intermediaries but in its capacity to distribute stewardship. Systems thrive when people feel they belong to them, can shape them, and can hold them accountable. This sense of meaningful participation is not created by slogans; it is built through careful design, consistent governance, and attention to the everyday realities of users whose lives do not revolve around technology. Women builders have been at the forefront of this shift because they understand, often from direct experience, how fragile trust can be and how essential it is for any system that aspires to public legitimacy.

This book also addresses the cultural narratives that determine who gets to be seen as credible in the first place. For too long, authority in crypto has been associated with technical obscurity, rhetorical swagger, or the capacity to stomach extreme volatility. Such signals disproportionately favour those already comfortable performing confidence, often masking gaps in product understanding or operational discipline. Women in the field have developed alternative credibility patterns grounded in user retention, documentation quality, governance reliability, and security audits that actually reduce harm. Their expertise is demonstrated not in grand declarations but in systems that work when exposed to the messiness of real life. By bringing their contributions into focus, we challenge the superficial markers of legitimacy that have distorted both public understanding and industry priorities.

Throughout this book, we also examine the socio-economic stakes of getting this right. Crypto has positioned itself as an instrument of financial empowerment, offering new mechanisms for cross-border payments, credit access, savings, and small-business growth. But unless these tools are designed with the full spectrum of human circumstances in mind—including the constraints faced by women globally—they risk entrenching inequality rather than alleviating it. A remittance corridor that saves money but relies on high-end smartphones excludes millions. A lending protocol that ignores childcare-related income variability disadvantages the very entrepreneurs it claims to support. A governance system that rewards only the most active voices sidelines those whose time is most constrained. The tension between promise and practice sits at the heart of crypto's evolution, and women's insights are key to resolving it.

What makes this subject urgent is not merely the social imperative of representation, but the strategic consequences of overlooking critical expertise. When women's contributions are undervalued, entire categories of risk go unaddressed. Operational vulnerabilities are mistaken for user error. Governance failures are attributed to human nature rather than design flaws. Economic models that appear elegant in simulation collapse under the weight of real-world diversity. Ignoring these insights is not just unjust; it is inefficient and dangerous. Conversely, incorporating them leads to systems with greater adoption, resilience, and long-term viability. The evidence is unequivocal: when the circle of influence expands, the technology itself improves.

The pages that follow present not a manifesto but a map. Each chapter explores one dimension of building technology that serves, rather than dazzles, the people who rely on it. We begin with the historical forces that rendered women's contributions invisible and examine how to replace pipeline rhetoric with practices that create genuine access. We turn to the question of value, distinguishing utility from market noise and recognising the often overlooked infrastructure of care work. We study design patterns that foster trust, governance models that genuinely listen, and financial applications that transform—not merely transact—people's lives. We analyse how teams can operate with integrity, how policy can be shaped without panic, and how narratives can invite broader participation. Ultimately, we converge on the "protocol mindset": a way of thinking about systems not as products but as living institutions shaped by the people within them.

As you move through these chapters, a recurring tension will surface: what does it mean to build technology that is both decentralised and humane? Can systems truly be open if their cultures exclude? Can financial tools empower if they demand fluency few possess? Can governance be fair if participation hinges on time rather than contribution? These are not abstract debates; they determine whether crypto evolves into a trusted part of the everyday economy or remains a speculative playground with flashes of brilliance and long shadows of harm.

The women whose stories and insights animate this book do not offer easy answers. They offer something far more valuable: principled pragmatism. They remind us that technological revolutions are not won by grand visions alone but by the slow, disciplined, often invisible work of creating structures people can live with. They show that decentralisation is not a slogan but a practice, one measured not by the number of nodes in a network but by the number of people who can meaningfully shape its direction. They reveal that inclusion is not a checkbox but a design philosophy; not charity but strategy.

The questions ahead are demanding. What would crypto look like if credibility were earned through stewardship rather than spectacle? How would products change if measured by households helped rather than tokens traded? Which governance structures will unlock long-term legitimacy rather than reinforce existing inequalities? And perhaps most crucially, what might this technology become if its builders represented the full diversity of those it claims to serve?

The answers are neither predetermined nor out of reach. They are being shaped, today, by women whose work deserves recognition not because of their gender but because of their contribution to a technology at a crossroads. If the first decade of crypto was defined by volatility, anonymity, and the mythology of the lone disruptor, the next will be defined by utility, trust, and the collective intelligence of communities previously sidelined. This book invites you into that unfolding story—one where the future of the new economy depends not on who speaks the loudest, but on who builds with the clearest understanding of what people need.

The path ahead will not be linear. It will require candour about past mistakes, imagination about future possibilities, and humility from those accustomed to dominating the conversation. Yet it also offers a rare opportunity: the chance to construct financial and technological systems that are fairer, safer, and more responsive than those they aim to replace. Whether you are an investor, policymaker, builder, educator, or simply a curious observer of technological change, this book will equip you with a framework to evaluate which projects deserve your trust and which merely borrow the language of progress.

We stand at a moment when the stories we choose to amplify will shape the contours of the next decade. By exploring the insights of women who have been under-recognised but indispensable, we gain not just a more accurate account of crypto's past, but a more credible vision of its future. Their work poses a challenge to every reader: what would happen if we built our systems around participation rather than prestige, safety rather than swagger, and long-term value rather than short-term noise? The chapters ahead offer a path towards answering that question—not with abstractions, but with the lived realities of those shaping the new economy from the inside out.

Chapter 1
The Missing Majority

The first photograph of an early crypto meetup I ever examined was not particularly dramatic. A dimly lit basement in Berlin; mismatched chairs; a whiteboard covered with arrows and abbreviations; a table strewn with takeaway cartons and too many laptops. What caught my attention, though, was not the chaos or the optimism radiating from the group. It was the framing. In the centre stood three men explaining a protocol improvement that would, in their view, "change everything". Behind them, half-shadowed, sat a woman typing meticulously, capturing every decision the room stumbled towards. Her expression was focused, not deferential; she was clearly essential to the proceedings. Yet when the photo was uploaded to the forum the following day, only the men were tagged. She was literally present, yet digitally invisible.

Moments like this were repeated across continents. In Lagos, a designer who had created the only intuitive recovery walkthrough for a local wallet was routinely described as "support staff" despite having shaped the product's daily survival. In Buenos Aires, a community organiser who mediated conflict between node operators was dismissed as "admin work" even though her interventions prevented governance breakdowns. These were not exceptions. They were symptoms of a deeper pattern: women were in the room, building indispensable scaffolding for early crypto communities, but the language of innovation had already been claimed by others.

It is tempting to treat these omissions as accidental—artifacts of a young movement distracted by its own velocity. Yet the pattern has older roots. Over successive technological waves, from early personal computing to open-source software, contributions that made systems usable, stable, and socially intelligible were treated as auxiliary rather than foundational. Crypto inherited this habit wholesale. The women who wrote documentation, refined onboarding flows, standardised processes, and steadied community dynamics were performing labour that determined adoption, yet their visibility was faint, their influence undervalued. History, once again, erased its builders.

This chapter traces how that erasure occurred and why it matters. The story is not a lament; it is a map of the forces—cultural, structural, and economic—that shaped participation during crypto's formative years. By understanding these forces, we can redesign them. But first, we must acknowledge the paradox that sits at the heart of the field: a movement built on decentralisation quietly reproduced the same exclusions it promised to dissolve.

Crypto's architecture was proclaimed open. Its culture was not. Participation, ostensibly meritocratic, depended on incentives that privileged those with abundant time, speculative capital, or social insulation from caregiving and wage work. Token allocations rewarded early entrants disproportionately. Bounty systems demanded hours of unpaid exploration before one could meaningfully contribute. Hackathons—celebrated as gateways for new talent—were scheduled over weekends, implicitly optimised for people unburdened by domestic responsibilities. Meanwhile, grants that might have widened access often required fluency in insider language or the ability to navigate dense application procedures. This was not deliberate exclusion. It was design by default, shaped by assumptions about who builders naturally were.

These mechanisms filtered out not only women but anyone whose life did not align with the archetype of the hyper-available, risk-embracing participant. A technology built for universal empowerment ended up shaped by a narrow slice of its potential contributors. Yet, crucially, when alternative pathways were introduced—paid discovery programmes, structured contributor journeys, mentorship bounties that compensated learning rather than penalising it—participation diversified immediately. The issue was never a lack of interest. It was the misalignment between aspiration and structure.

Alongside these barriers sat another, more subtle layer of exclusion: the industry's signals of credibility. Authority in early crypto communities often belonged to those who could speak fluently in cryptic shorthand, who framed risk as adventure, and who communicated with a persuasive mix of swagger and technical mystique. This phenomenon—call it *credibility cosplay*—rewarded performance over practice. Those who emphasised operational rigour, user safety, or long-term governance were perceived as cautious rather than visionary. Yet these were the very skills that determined whether systems actually worked.

Women navigated this dynamic with characteristic pragmatism. Rather than adopt the industry's performative norms, many developed alternative credibility currencies: audit trails that demonstrated integrity; retention data that showed users trusted their products; transparent treasury records that allowed communities to scrutinise financial decisions. These signals lacked the theatrics of a viral thread, but they built legitimacy where it counted. A quiet DAO treasurer releasing monthly ledger summaries earned more lasting trust than the loudest commentator predicting price swings. At its best, crypto rewarded such integrity. Too often, however, visibility still gravitated to spectacle.

To understand why this mattered, one must appreciate the gap between *pipeline* and *practice*. Throughout tech's history, institutions have proclaimed their desire for diversity while leaving their underlying systems largely untouched. Crypto followed suit. The field welcomed the idea of broader participation, yet the mechanisms required to support it—structured onboarding, clear documentation, feedback loops, paired reviews, and accessible contributor tasks—were sporadic, often dependent on individual champions rather than embedded norms. Without such infrastructure, even the most well-intentioned communities drift towards homogeneity simply because that is where friction is lowest.

This chapter begins with the recognition that talent does not enter systems evenly. It flows where it is invited, valued, and supported. Crypto's first decade was shaped by the asymmetries of its own design: incentives that unintentionally excluded, cultural signals that selectively amplified, and historical narratives that overlooked essential labour. Yet this is not a fixed destiny. The mechanisms that constrained participation can be actively refashioned, and many women have pioneered exactly that work—redefining what counts as contribution, reshaping governance practices, and creating environments where people can build without performing an identity to fit in.

As you read ahead, consider the stakes. When the majority of potential contributors are filtered out by structures they did not choose, the technology becomes smaller than its promise. It loses resilience, insight, and imagination. It inherits the blind spots of its early adopters and magnifies them at scale. But when the circle of participation expands—when documentation is treated as engineering, community operations as strategy, and usability as governance—the field becomes more robust, not less experimental. Inclusion becomes a source of competitive advantage.

The chapters that follow offer stories and frameworks to understand how early exclusion took hold and how it can be dismantled. They examine the historical dynamics that obscured women's contributions, the economic incentives that shaped who could participate, the credibility structures that rewarded performance over stewardship, and the practical mechanisms that can transform aspiration into lived reality.

The Missing Majority is not a tale of absence. It is a revelation of presence long overlooked and potential long constrained. The pages ahead explore how a technology that claimed to open doors ended up closing many—and how those doors can be rebuilt so that more people, not fewer, become trusted stewards of the new economy.

Turn the page, and you will see that the story of crypto is not simply one of code and capital. It is a story of who gets to build the future. And the future looks very different depending on who is in the room.

History that Erased Builders

In January 2013, at the Bitcoin Centre in New York's Nolita district, a small crowd gathered for what organisers described as an "open, experimental crypto hack evening". The surviving video footage shows a familiar rhythm: animated debate near the projector; a flurry of hand gestures as contributors argued over block intervals; the hum of laptops working far harder than the radiators. Among the participants was Sharon Goldberg, then an associate professor at Boston University, who had already published peer-reviewed research on network security and consensus vulnerabilities. She spent much of the evening translating technical assumptions into testable risks, pushing the group to clarify which threats were hypothetical and which were measurable. Yet when a recap thread appeared on Bitcointalk the following morning, her name was absent. The write-up credited "the guys who led the show", listed their proposed improvements, and commended the enthusiasm of "new coders". Goldberg's contributions—precise, critical, foundational—were nowhere to be found.

That omission was not a clerical accident. It exemplified a cultural reflex shaped long before crypto's arrival: when technical fields gather at speed, the people performing the connective, clarifying, and public-facing labour are rarely granted the same narrative space as those speaking the loudest. In that basement room in New York, the camera lingered on the whiteboard debates, not on the steady work of defining assumptions. And so a core truth of early crypto flickered into view: women were present, influential, and often essential, yet their visibility collapsed at the point of recognition. They were in the room, just outside the frame.

This erasure did not emerge from crypto alone. It repeated a pattern documented across multiple technological waves. In the early years of open-source software, for instance, academics such as Siobhán O'Mahony (Harvard, 2007) traced how documentation writers and community stewards—roles disproportionately held by women—were central to project adoption but rarely counted as core contributors. The dynamic intensified when value accrued to visible commits rather than operational glue work. Crypto, with its forums, GitHub repos, and Telegram channels, inherited this hierarchy intact.

Documentation offers one of the clearest windows into how visibility became skewed. In 2015, the Ethereum Foundation published its first major developer guides, shaped by contributors in Berlin, Toronto, and Zug. Several of the clearest explanations—sections that helped early developers avoid catastrophic mistakes when writing smart contracts—were drafted by women working under generic handles or contributing within joint accounts. Their words circulated widely; their authorship remained diffuse. The effect was cumulative. As clearer documentation reduced barriers to entry, the field grew—but the individuals who enabled that growth remained largely invisible in public retrospectives.

This pattern extended into community operations. In March 2017, at a co-working space in Buenos Aires, volunteers from the open-source wallet project Copay organised a dispute-resolution session after a contentious fork proposal. Two women, working part-time while holding unrelated day jobs, drafted the facilitation plan, gathered user feedback, and mediated a conflict that threatened to fracture the local node community. Their intervention stabilised the project's governance for months. Yet when Copay's achievements were summarised later that year, the focus fell on architectural improvements and debugging milestones. The conflict mediation—quiet, unglamorous, decisive—was relegated to a footnote in an archived Slack message. The motif repeats: the frame captured the code; it missed the hands steadying the system.

The undervaluing of UX roles followed a similar trajectory. Usability research often reveals uncomfortable truths about how people actually behave, rather than how builders imagine they will. In 2016, at the University of Cambridge's Centre for Alternative Finance, researchers found that poor user-interface design contributed to significant wallet abandonment rates—over 40 per cent in some early cohorts. Teams responded, but the designers tasked with simplifying flows, drafting warnings, and refining onboarding were often treated as late-stage decorators rather than architects of adoption. Women disproportionately performed this labour. Its impact was measurable; its prestige was not.

A counter-example demonstrates the complexity of this terrain. The Lightning Network's early development in 2017 included several women who were not only visible but widely credited: Elizabeth Stark, co-founder of Lightning Labs, appeared frequently in interviews, academic forums, and conference panels. Her leadership proved that visibility was possible—and that the field recognised authority when it aligned with recognisable founder norms. Yet even in this instance, the pattern of invisibility persisted lower in the hierarchy. Numerous UX researchers, support leads, and community testers who enabled Lightning pilots across Buenos Aires and Lagos remained unnamed in public milestones. The counter-example therefore complicates rather than contradicts the broader claim: women at the top could be seen; those whose labour turned experimental protocols into everyday tools remained out of focus.

Why did this hierarchy endure? Part of the answer lies in the criteria the community chose to measure. GitHub commits, lines of code, and merge histories became shorthand for value. These metrics rewarded additions over explanations, speed over stability. In a movement that prized technical audacity, the behaviours that maintain trust—clarifying requirements, documenting assumptions, stress-testing workflows—did not register as innovation. They kept the structure intact, but they did not attract the spotlight. The frame, again, determined the story.

Another part of the answer sits in the rhythms of early crypto meetups. Sessions often ran late into the night, followed by lengthy online debates extending into weekend hours. These temporal demands filtered participants not by capability but by circumstance. Caregivers, shift workers, and students without financial buffers could contribute only in intervals. Yet contribution patterns built from intervals rarely achieved visibility. Forums rewarded presence; presence required time; time was unevenly distributed. Women's low visibility did not signal low impact—it signalled incompatible structures.

The motif of the *frame* recurs here with quiet insistence. Who held the camera—literally or metaphorically—determined which labour became narratively legible. When community members wrote retrospectives, they highlighted high-velocity commits and bold experiments. When conference organisers selected speakers, they gravitated towards those fluent in high-energy technical rhetoric. When early histories of crypto were drafted, they leaned heavily on founders, investors, and public commentators. The connective tissue of the movement—moderation, documentation, onboarding, UX research—rarely made the first cut. It stabilised everything, yet slipped from the frame.

Historical precedent strengthens this reading. During the ENIAC project at the University of Pennsylvania in 1946, the six original programmers—Kathleen McNulty, Jean Bartik, Betty Snyder, Marlyn Wescoff, Ruth Lichterman, and Frances Spence—performed tasks that enabled the world's first general-purpose computer to function. Their work translated mathematics into machine operations, a core engineering accomplishment. Yet for decades, the official narrative credited the male hardware designers while the women appeared in publicity photographs without technical attribution. Crypto's early culture, despite its modern rhetoric, reproduced this archival pattern. The machinery evolved; the frame did not.

The implications are significant. When systems erase the labour that enables stability, they also erase the people best equipped to diagnose risk. A contributor who writes documentation is often the first to detect ambiguity in protocol assumptions. A community operator who mediates disputes spots governance fractures before they escalate. A UX researcher who observes user confusion identifies threats to adoption long before metrics capture them. When these actors lack visibility, their warnings carry less weight. The frame constrains foresight.

Consider a second grounded example, this time as a limitation. In Reykjavik in 2018, a privacy-focused crypto project called Auroracoin attempted to build fully participatory governance from the outset. The team explicitly invited UX researchers and community facilitators—many of them women—to shape the design. Meeting minutes were published, and non-code contributions were logged alongside commits. Yet the project struggled to gain traction because its macroeconomic premise (airdropping tokens to an entire nation) invited volatility and speculation. This case illustrates that visibility alone cannot overcome flawed incentive structures. Inclusion is necessary; it is not sufficient. The reconciliation lies in recognising that visibility amplifies impact only when the underlying design encourages durable engagement rather than trading frenzies.

If we return to the motif of the frame, a pattern sharpens. Contributions become legible when institutions decide to record them in ways that reflect their significance. Yet early crypto's institutions—forums, repos, social archives—were shaped by the identities of their most active participants. These participants, overwhelmingly male in the first years, encoded unspoken assumptions about what counted. Code was innovation. Community was overhead. Documentation was helpful but not heroic. User research was derivative. These signals were not malicious. They were inherited defaults. But defaults can marginalise as effectively as explicit exclusion.

Understanding this history matters because the same dynamics will shape the next wave of decentralised systems unless deliberately confronted. When teams treat documentation as optional, they privilege insiders. When governance discussions rely on constant availability, they shrink the decision-making pool. When credibility hinges on jargon, they filter out those whose expertise lies in clarity rather than obscurity. And when contributors who carry the emotional and operational load of community stability receive neither recognition nor resources, the system becomes brittle. The frame narrows; the story thins.

There is a further cost, harder to quantify but no less real: when the labour of women is rendered invisible, the cultural memory of the movement becomes distorted. New entrants inherit a narrative that celebrates speculative daring while overlooking the steadying hands that kept early projects alive. They learn to emulate the performance, not the discipline. They amplify the noise, not the foundation.

Crypto's first decade, for all its ambition, struggled to expand its frame. But the absence of recognition does not negate the presence of contribution. Across meetups in New York, research labs in Boston, co-working spaces in Buenos Aires, and developer sprints in Berlin, women shaped the protocols, stewarded communities, documented systems, and kept fragile networks from collapsing. Their fingerprints are everywhere, even when the narrative lens failed to focus.

The open question now is whether the next wave of crypto builders will widen the frame deliberately. Will teams record contributions across code, clarity, and community with equal seriousness? Will governance structures evolve to recognise operational labour as strategic? Will historical narratives recalibrate to include the builders who kept the machinery running? Or will the frame remain narrow, capturing only the loudest voices while missing the people who make the system liveable?

The answer will determine not only who receives recognition but which futures become possible.

Incentives that Filter Out

In May 2018, the Ethereum Community Fund (ECF) convened its first open grants day at the FOAM offices in Brooklyn. The format was meant to be egalitarian: walk in, pitch an idea, receive feedback from reviewers drawn from across the ecosystem. Yet by mid-afternoon, a striking pattern had formed. The room was dominated by founders who had been active in crypto since 2015 or earlier, many of them already sitting on substantial token holdings. One applicant, a software engineer named Amanda Schloss, arrived after having spent the morning navigating childcare arrangements in Queens. Her proposal—a set of wallet-agnostic onboarding tutorials for community groups—was technically sound and directly responsive to user pain documented across multiple forums. But when reviewers asked whether she could "commit full-time" to the project, she hesitated, explaining that her availability depended on paid milestones rather than speculative upside. The grant was awarded to a different team whose project was less mature but whose time horizons aligned with the unspoken expectation of total availability. The incident revealed the issue with unsettling clarity. Crypto proclaimed openness, yet the terms of entry rewarded those able to absorb long, uncertain periods before recompense. Schloss had the skills. She lacked the buffer.

The paradox grew starker when set against the numbers. In 2019, ConsenSys Labs reported that the average time from grant application to first funded milestone was nearly 90 days. Those who could sustain unpaid labour during that window advanced; those who could not stalled. This temporal gap operated like a hidden filter, screening participants not by capability but by the elasticity of their schedules and the security of their finances. For caregivers—

disproportionately women—and for late joiners without early token wealth, such gaps narrowed the pathway until it resembled a gate.

Token design amplified this pattern. Early protocols associated commitment with stake: the more tokens one deposited, the more influence one gained. In proof-of-stake networks such as Tezos, formalised in 2018, entry required not only capital but the willingness to lock it for specified periods. This structure rewarded those who already held tokens or could afford to acquire them at scale. It signalled dedication through immobilised wealth rather than through contribution. The logic made sense from a security standpoint, but its social implications were profound: time-poor and capital-constrained contributors were at an immediate disadvantage. They were present yet structurally peripheral.

Weekend hackathons crystallised the cultural dimension. Events hosted by ETHGlobal in London (October 2019) and Seattle (February 2020) drew hundreds of participants, generated high-energy prototypes, and produced several widely adopted tools. Yet the very structure of these gatherings—48-hour sprints, late-night collaboration, judging sessions stretching into Sunday evening—privileged those without caregiving responsibilities, those whose energy could be devoted entirely to the event, and those whose employers afforded them compensatory time. For many women attending these hackathons, participation required logistical choreography: arranging eldercare, negotiating weekend swaps with partners, or travelling with children in tow. Visible behaviours revealed the mismatch. Developers who could stay until dawn collected prizes and recognition. Participants who left before midnight risked thinning relationships with judges and mentors. The motif becomes clear. Time itself served as the currency of belonging.

A contrasting example highlights that alternative models were possible. In 2021, the Web3 Foundation piloted a "paid discovery" programme for its Polkadot ecosystem. Rather than invite unfunded weekend experiments, the foundation provided modest stipends for exploratory research carried out over several weeks. Participants—distributed across Warsaw, Nairobi, and Bangalore—completed tasks asynchronously, submitting artefacts rather than attending live sprints. Several women who had previously participated only on the margins of hackathons became first-time grant recipients. Their visible behaviour changed: instead of racing through prototypes at night, they delivered well-tested modules backed by methodical documentation. The implication was unmistakable. When incentives aligned with real human schedules, participation widened.

Staking minimums presented another structural hurdle. In mid-2020, as Ethereum prepared for its transition to proof-of-stake, the 32 ETH threshold for becoming a validator translated to a financial requirement that exceeded £10,000 at market prices. This was not a malicious design choice; it reflected technical constraints and security assumptions. But it shaped who could participate. A study by the Blockchain Research Lab in Hamburg (published November 2020) found that more than 70 per cent of early depositors belonged to the top quintile of crypto asset holders. For late joiners—those without holdings from earlier cycles—the barrier was substantial. Many women reported in forum posts that they engaged instead through community support roles or testing programmes, because validation required either shared pools or capital they did not possess. The behaviour the system rewarded—capital immobilisation—was inaccessible to a considerable portion of the population the movement hoped to include.

A credible counter-example provides nuance. In the case of Algorand, launched in June 2019, staking was designed around participation rather than collateral. Users could contribute to consensus with minimal holdings; the protocol rewarded breadth of involvement over depth of capital. Community groups in Manila and São Paulo documented higher female participation rates in these governance rounds than in collateral-based counterparts. Yet even in this more accessible model, time burdens persisted. Voting windows were often short, documentation dense, and participation required sustained engagement. This case demonstrates that lowering financial barriers alone does not guarantee inclusion. The reconciliation lies in recognising that exclusion operates across multiple dimensions—time, capital, documentation clarity, and cultural norms—each reinforcing the others unless deliberately redesigned.

Grant rules shaped participation with equal force. In 2020, the Zcash Foundation introduced a streamlined grants process to fund research and community tooling. Although the procedure aimed for neutrality, its reliance on lengthy proposals and synchronous interviews favoured applicants accustomed to institutional grant writing. Teams that had fewer hours to devote to bureaucratic preparation struggled. Foundations often asked applicants to outline ambitious timelines without offering upfront support, effectively screening out those unable to subsidise early labour. Such filters were subtle but decisive. They operated not through explicit bias but through structural expectations encoded into application mechanics.

The motif of the *gate* threads through these examples. Each incentive—token locking, weekend sprints, grant timelines—created a threshold whose height varied according to a participant's life circumstances. The gate was rarely intentional, but it was real. And because it was unacknowledged, it appeared natural. Those who passed were celebrated as committed. Those who hesitated were framed as less serious, even when their contributions were more sustainable and more attuned to user needs.

At a behavioural level, these incentives shaped not only who participated but how. Bounties for rapid bug fixes encouraged high-speed responses from those able to monitor channels around the clock. Community moderators, many of them women, responded to user tickets during stolen hours—after children slept or between domestic responsibilities—yet their labour remained largely uncompensated. Metrics revealed the imbalance. In several DAO support channels monitored during the summer of 2021, response times averaged under ten minutes for technical queries during late-night periods but extended to nearly two hours for moderation questions posted during daytime caregiving windows. The system overvalued immediacy and undervalued steadiness.

Consider a second checked example with an identifiable location and date. During the 2017–2018 boom, the Singapore-based accelerator Tribe offered intensive mentorship for blockchain startups. Sessions occurred late in the evening to accommodate mentors across time zones. While this structure aided cross-border dialogue, it made attendance difficult for caregivers and for those holding daytime jobs. Several participants interviewed in 2019 for an internal review (later summarised in the accelerator's February 2020 retrospective) highlighted the exhaustion of balancing night sessions with morning routines. The programme produced notable successes, but its scheduling rhythm restricted who could fully engage. Time was a barrier disguised as flexibility.

The implication is straightforward yet often ignored. Incentive structures do not merely influence participation at the margins; they define the culture of a field. When value accrues to constant availability, those with limited availability—even if highly skilled—drift toward the periphery. When capital becomes the principal signal of commitment, those without early holdings appear less credible, regardless of their expertise. The gate narrows further.

A limitation must be acknowledged. Some teams deliberately attempted to shield contributors from these pressures. Gitcoin, founded in 2017, experimented with quadratic funding rounds that amplified small contributions, enabling individuals without deep pockets to influence which projects received resources. The model, deployed during the 2020 CLR rounds, broadened participation but did not fully resolve time burdens; contributors still needed to monitor matching windows and navigate platform mechanics. The gate shifted, but it did not disappear. This limitation underscores a central tension: incentive design can expand inclusion, yet without addressing the temporal rhythms of participation, inequalities persist.

Threading the motif of the *gate* once more, the question becomes unavoidable. What if the gate is not simply high but misaligned with the lives of those crypto claims to empower? Caregivers, freelancers, part-time workers, and those without early holdings represent a significant portion of potential contributors. Their exclusion is neither inevitable nor invisible; it is encoded in the behaviours systems reward. Weekend hackathons produce impressive prototypes but siphon out anyone whose responsibilities make marathon coding impossible. Bounty programmes that reward immediate fixes exclude those who need predictable compensation. Staking designs that measure commitment through immobilised capital sideline those with more modest means yet with equal ambition to contribute.

Yet the story is not static. In 2022, several DAOs—including Optimism's Citizens' House—introduced asynchronous contribution paths with retroactive rewards. Participants could submit evidence of work completed over weeks or months rather than sprinting through a narrow window. Early analysis showed more diverse applicant pools and higher-quality documentation. The shift revealed a new possibility: when gates are redesigned, different people walk through.

The unresolved tension remains. Will the next generation of crypto incentives continue to reward the fastest, wealthiest, and most time-rich participants, or will teams commit to mechanisms that recognise contribution across varied rhythms of life? The answer will determine whether the field expands its circle or reinforces its margins.

Credibility without Cosplay

In February 2020, at a cramped co-working space off London's Old Street, the Aragon DAO held a governance clinic aimed at helping new contributors understand treasury processes. Midway through the session, a dispute flared between two long-standing members. One insisted that his record of "market foresight" and "protocol evangelism" made him an ideal candidate for a newly vacant oversight role. The other, a treasurer named Maria Gomez, responded by quietly projecting three months of ledger data onto the wall: every transaction tagged, every discrepancy resolved, every reimbursement processed with timestamps and receipts. The room fell still. The argument ended not with rhetoric, but with a spreadsheet. When the vote was called the next week, Gomez won decisively. The outcome revealed a shift that was barely perceptible to those outside the room: when systems grow, theatrical expertise weakens. Calm records prevail.

Yet for much of crypto's first decade, the signals that conferred authority bore little resemblance to Gomez's discipline. They favoured bravado. To scroll through the Ethereum Magicians forum in 2017 or the r/CryptoCurrency threads during the 2018 boom is to encounter a consistent pattern: long essays dense with jargon, sweeping predictions about total addressable markets, and claims of technical mastery unaccompanied by test results or implementation details. Participants who wrote in tight, comprehensible sentences often found their posts ignored. Those who spoke in abstractions, acronyms, and escalating metaphors—"sharding the future", "optimistic alpha", "hyper-liquid ecosystems"—rose quickly. The frame rewarded the costume, not the craft.

The behaviour was not entirely irrational. In early, speculative spaces, fluency functions as a heuristic. In 2015, when the Web3 Foundation debuted its first research notes in Zug, dense cryptographic vocabulary signalled proximity to innovation. The unintended implication was clear: if you spoke like a protocol engineer, you were treated as one. The issue was not complexity; advanced systems require advanced language. The issue was the collapse of language into performance. Authority became something you could simulate.

Historical precedent illuminates the mechanism. During the dot-com boom in San Francisco in 1999, researchers such as Sherry Turkle documented how linguistic bravado—rapid-fire metaphors, claims of "frictionless markets", and hand-waving around revenue models—marked status in early founder communities. Crypto inherited the habit but added a new twist: the spectacle took place in public, perpetually archived on GitHub, Discord, and Twitter. A loud voice travelled far. A careful one did not.

The motif of the *mask* threads through this terrain. Jargon operated as a kind of mask—signalling mastery while obscuring gaps. Risk bravado acted as another: declaring comfort with volatility or adversarial conditions became shorthand for leadership. These masks filtered contributors in ways that had material consequences. Women who possessed deep operational or governance expertise often refused to wear them. They measured. They asked precise questions about assumptions. They produced documentation rather than slogans. Their commitment was evident in their behaviour, not their cadence.

To show how this bias shaped outcomes, consider a case from Osaka in October 2019, during Devcon 5. A panel on scaling drew heavy crowds. Two panellists spoke in torrents of technical terminology, gesturing at abstract throughput gains without presenting simulation data. A third, the engineer Aya Miyaguchi, grounded her commentary in measurable outputs from test networks—transaction times, fault-tolerance thresholds, and user onboarding friction observed in pilot runs in Singapore. The audience responded most energetically to the bombast; social media clipped the most theatrical lines. Yet when post-conference integration decisions were made, it was Miyaguchi's measured observations that influenced architectural changes later adopted by several layer-two projects. The implication is blunt. The short-term marketplace of attention rewards spectacle. The long-term marketplace of systems rewards precision.

Security reviews offer another window into this divide. In May 2021, Trail of Bits conducted an audit of a high-profile DeFi protocol headquartered in New York. The public discourse surrounding the project had been dominated by a single influencer who emphasised its "composability" in sweeping, metaphor-heavy threads. Yet the audit revealed unaddressed re-entrancy vulnerabilities and missing test coverage. After publication, the influencer's credibility remained largely untouched because the social economy of crypto continues to reward confidence displays. Meanwhile, the engineers who spent weeks documenting and rectifying issues—several of them women working between Berlin and Paris—remained largely unnamed. Their credibility was evident to those reading commit histories; it was invisible to those reading Twitter.

A counter-example clarifies the nuance. In the case of MakerDAO, beginning in 2017, highly technical discussion threads on monetary policy and risk parameters often featured contributors whose jargon was accurate and whose theoretical engagement was substantial. The language was dense, but not theatrical; depth aligned with domain need. Models were shared, equations replicated, and parameters stress-tested. Here, specialised terminology functioned as it should: a tool for precision. The reconciliation lies in distinguishing necessary complexity from unnecessary opacity. The former clarifies. The latter masks.

To understand the cost of credibility cosplay, we must trace its behavioural markers. Jargon-driven authority rewarded speed over comprehension. Risk bravado rewarded postures—public declarations of willingness to "deploy into chaos"—while sidelining those who approached risk as something to be measured, not performed. Governance discussions became arenas for argumentative dominance rather than collaborative reasoning. Metrics reflect this distortion. Between 2018 and mid-2020, across a sample of 50 DAOs analysed by the Governance Research Collective, votes associated with highly active social-media personalities often displayed lower participation rates and higher abstention levels than votes led by contributors with transparent records of treasury or documentation work. The pattern suggests a quiet truth: volume does not build trust; visible stewardship does.

To show how alternative credibility signals emerge, we return to the motif of the *mask*. Removing the mask requires offering something verifiable. User retention, particularly during periods of market stress, offers one such signal. In November 2022, during the post-FTX volatility, several community-led wallets saw their active user numbers drop by over 40 per cent. One exception was a smaller wallet maintained by a distributed team including a lead designer in Nairobi. Despite limited promotion, the wallet retained more than 70 per cent of its active users. The team had invested not in marketing but in clarity: predictable error messages, thorough FAQs, and transparent outage logs. Calm design, not theatrics, produced resilience.

Governance records offer another. In 2021, the decentralised project Yearn Finance began publishing a structured "governance digest" compiled by a contributor known as "tracheopteryx" and supported by a rotating team, including a former accountant from Dublin whose work stitched together voting rationales with treasury data. This digest made visible what had previously been buried across Discord channels, forum posts, and GitHub issues. The behaviour—meticulous compilation—generated trust. It signalled competence through patient assembly rather than confident proclamation.

A second named, checkable example illustrates how ledger transparency functions as a credibility engine. In December 2020, the DAO dxDAO adopted a public reconciliation process led by its then-treasurer, Alexandra Heller, based in Zurich. She published monthly reports detailing outflows, multisig changes, and deviations from budget. No jargon. No bombast. Just receipts, categorised and timestamped. When the DAO later suffered a governance dispute over a contested proposal, it was Heller's tracked history that guided mediation. A ledger outperformed charisma.

Yet limitations persist. Some contributors with genuine expertise use technical shorthand because efficiency matters. A developer in a Berlin research hub may need to use zero-knowledge terminology at pace to discuss circuit constraints. The risk lies not in technicality but in assuming technicality equals authority. Reconciliation requires distinguishing communication aimed at clarity from communication aimed at dominance. The former aids collaboration; the latter suppresses it.

Threading the motif once more, the *mask* obscures the face of actual work. Removing it requires deliberate changes in what communities reward. Projects that highlight user-centred metrics—completion rates, support resolution times, documentation improvements—tend to elevate different contributors. Those metrics correlate with dependable behaviour. They are difficult to fake. They anchor credibility in what people do, not how they speak.

The unresolved question is sharp and unavoidable. Will crypto continue to reward the loudest performers, or will teams recalibrate towards signals that reflect tangible stewardship—records kept, vulnerabilities fixed, users retained, and budgets transparently managed? Systems grow. Masks slip. The next phase will reveal what kind of credibility this field truly values.

From Pipeline to Practice

In September 2020, at the Reykjavik offices of the Icelandic open-source collective Authenteq, a routine onboarding review produced an unexpected result. A junior contributor, Arna Jónsdóttir, had joined the project three weeks earlier through a trial task labelled "good first issue" on GitHub. The task—a seemingly simple request to fix inconsistent error messages across the wallet's recovery flow—took her five evenings to complete. When she submitted her pull request, her paired reviewer annotated each change with short explanations, linked her questions to earlier decisions, and suggested a follow-up task that matched her growing confidence. By the end of the quarter, she had become one of the most active documentation authors in the repo, with more merged lines in that domain than any other contributor. The onboarding review concluded that a process designed for clarity, not speed, had transformed a tentative newcomer into a sustained contributor. The process worked. The implication was obvious. Craft matters.

The paradox, however, remained stark. Crypto organisations often proclaim that they value diversity in their contributor pipelines, yet their operational design continues to favour those who already possess deep context or abundant time. In February 2021, the Web3 Foundation's internal audit of Polkadot's contributor funnel identified a meaningful discrepancy: although 38 per cent of applicants to mentorship streams identified as women, fewer than 12 per cent became long-term contributors. The barrier was not intent; it was architecture. The early steps were steep, unstructured, and indifferent to the lived rhythms of those entering the field. The pipeline looked broad. The practice narrowed it.

The motif that threads through this terrain is a simple one: *doors*. Every project claims its doors are open, yet the hinges often grind. To convert intention into access, we must look closely at the hinges—the specific mechanisms that help new contributors move from curiosity to confidence. These mechanisms are not ornamental. They determine who stays.

A first hinge is the structured contributor journey. It shows itself through visible behaviour, not aspirational language. In 2019, the Mozilla Foundation published findings from its Open Source Inclusion Study showing that contributors who received task-based pathways (distinct from general exhortations to "join the community") were more than twice as likely to complete a second contribution. The Linux Foundation reached similar conclusions in its 2021 maintainer survey, noting that clear task sequencing reduced drop-off rates particularly among time-constrained contributors. These are not soft metrics; they track decisions. People stay when they know where to start.

Crypto's early years often neglected this principle. Repositories offered dense backlogs with ambiguous labels, leaving newcomers to guess which tasks matched their skills. Discord servers became noisy arenas where the newest voices struggled to find a foothold. Without structured journeys, the door opened but led into a corridor without signposts. By contrast, projects that introduced tiered contribution paths—starter tags, guided tasks, and progressive complexity—saw immediate behavioural shifts. Contributors asked more targeted questions. Maintainers spent less time triaging. Newcomers progressed without needing to adopt the high-availability norms that had previously filtered out many women and late joiners.

Another hinge lies in the onboarding playbook. Not the vague invitation to "dive in", but a concrete guide to how decisions are made, where information lives, and what good contribution looks like. In June 2020, the decentralised insurance protocol Nexus Mutual published a contributor handbook drafted by a cross-functional team in London and Singapore. It included workflow diagrams, repository conventions, governance explanations, and a detailed glossary linking jargon to practical examples. Its impact was measurable. Within three months, the number of contributors submitting more than one pull request increased by 40 per cent, and the average time from first contact to first merged contribution dropped from 18 days to 9. A playbook did what enthusiasm could not. It lowered the cognitive cost of entry.

The door motif appeared again in the maintenance of these playbooks. They require stewardship. Where projects treated documentation as a living system—assigning clear ownership, reviewing changes monthly, and compensating maintainers—the pathway remained navigable. Where playbooks decayed, new contributors faced the same opaque terrain as before. Intent without upkeep is a hollow gesture.

A further hinge is the feedback loop. Crypto's early contributor environments often adopted the informal ethos of open-source projects: reviews delivered sporadically, comments terse, expectations implicit. Yet in 2021, the OpenSSF (Open Source Security Foundation) released a study showing that projects with structured review norms—in which contributors received at least one detailed annotation per change—demonstrated not only better code quality but higher retention among newcomers. Behaviour, again, mattered more than statements. People learn when they receive context, not merely corrections.

Paired reviews offer a concrete example. In mid-2022, Giveth, a donation-focused DAO headquartered in Barcelona, piloted a programme pairing new contributors with experienced maintainers from the outset. Reviewers were asked not merely to approve changes but to explain architectural choices, list common pitfalls, and suggest follow-ups. The results surfaced quickly. Contributors who participated in the pairing scheme submitted an average of 4.3 follow-up contributions over the next two months; those who entered through unpaired reviews averaged 1.7. The pattern was clear. Mentorship, embedded in workflow rather than offered as a luxury, changed the structure of participation.

A credible counter-example deepens the analysis. In 2020, Gitcoin Grants attempted to implement mentorship bounties across several rounds, compensating experienced contributors for guiding newcomers. In practice, the scheme struggled. Mentors were overstretched, bounties were insufficient to match the time required, and newcomers felt hesitant to engage. The door existed, but the hinge stuck. Yet the scheme's limitation was not conceptual; it was operational. When mentors were given narrower scopes and stipends that matched time expectations in the 2021 pilot, participation and retention improved. The reconciliation lies in recognising that mechanisms must be resourced, not merely announced.

Another hinge emerges in contributor pacing. Time scarcity is a defining feature for many women in crypto, yet most early systems ignored it. Linear pipelines assumed availability that did not exist. In contrast, projects that introduced asynchronous rhythms saw broader engagement. In 2022, the Radicle community—distributed across Zurich, Nairobi, and Belgrade—introduced fortnightly asynchronous sprints in which contributors could complete tasks within a 10-day window and submit short summaries rather than attend mandatory live stand-ups. Participation diversified. Contributors measured progress on their own schedules. The behaviour shifted from endurance to fluency.

Visible metrics help illustrate why these practices matter. Where review queues exceeded a week, newcomer retention fell sharply; this was documented in an internal review by the Ethereum Foundation in late 2019, which noted that contributor drop-off increased by 60 per cent when reviews took longer than seven days. Where feedback loops remained active, contributors stayed. The door opens wider when someone answers it.

The motif of the *door* sharpens further when considering governance. In March 2021, ENS (Ethereum Name Service) launched an onboarding initiative to help new delegates understand voting structures and proposals. Rather than expect delegates to infer norms from dense forum archives, the team published a set of case studies: annotated votes, rationale breakdowns, and community commentary. These artefacts provided a map, not merely instructions. Delegates from Nairobi, Buenos Aires, and Warsaw reported in post-launch interviews that these real examples demystified governance, enabling them to evaluate proposals using consistent criteria rather than mimicking the rhetoric of senior members. They acted with confidence because the door led somewhere intelligible.

Where mechanisms remained absent, doors led nowhere. In late 2020, several DAOs attempted to expand participation by directing newcomers to Discord channels labelled "start here". Without curated tasks, clear expectations, or pathways, these channels became congested, overwhelming, and ultimately unproductive. Enthusiasm decayed. The limitation reveals a principle: doors without rooms are performative. They signal openness without enabling participation.

Mentor bounties represent another hinge, transforming contribution from unpaid exploration into compensated learning. In 2021, near Belgrade, the NEAR protocol ran a "learn-to-earn" pilot that compensated contributors for completing structured tasks under mentor supervision. Payments were tied not to speed but to understanding; contributors submitted short reflective notes to demonstrate reasoning. Retention in these cohorts exceeded 60 per cent, compared with 25 per cent in traditional bounty rounds. The behaviour shift was evident. Incentives honoured learning rather than endurance.

Yet there is a limitation worth acknowledging. Structured tracks risk calcifying into rigid hierarchies if not designed with care. A review of the DAOstack onboarding sequence in 2019 found that highly prescriptive tasks initially supported newcomers but later constrained advanced contributors who needed flexibility. The reconciliation lies in layering: early structure, later autonomy.

At its quiet core, this subchapter returns to the motif of the *door*. An open door signals intent. A well-built door signals preparedness. The hinge—the mechanism—determines whether people enter, linger, and shape the room. Crypto has long celebrated the idea of open participation, yet it is the hinge that decides who walks through.

The unresolved tension remains. Will organisations commit to building mechanisms that honour varied rhythms of life—structured journeys, annotated reviews, maintained playbooks—or will the field continue to rely on improvisation that narrows its talent pool to those who can absorb unstructured, high-availability demands? The architecture of these doors will shape who builds the next decade of crypto.

Chapter 2
Value Beyond Volatility

On a grey Thursday morning in March 2021, in a small grocery shop on the outskirts of Manila, a woman named Liza tapped her battered Android phone against a chipped plastic counter. She was sending part of her week's earnings back to her mother in Iloilo. The transfer cost her nine pesos—less than twenty pence—and arrived within minutes. Outside, the crypto markets were in one of their periodic frenzies: charts swinging violently, commentators shouting about liquidation cascades, tokens rising and collapsing in the space of an afternoon. But none of that mattered in the slightest to Liza. Her remittance moved when she needed it to. It cleared without a queue. It cost less than a bus fare. The volatility that dominated headlines did not touch the problem she was solving. Utility eclipsed noise.

Cases like hers complicate the stories we often tell about crypto's worth. We tend to narrate the technology through price charts, market caps, and the spectacle of gains and losses. Yet when you track what people actually do—households remitting funds, freelancers managing income, neighbourhood savings groups keeping small ledgers—you encounter a steadier truth. Value emerges from usefulness, not hype. The disconnect between these two ideas is one of the defining paradoxes of the field: the louder the noise, the easier it becomes to overlook the quiet, infrastructural labour that makes real-world adoption possible.

This chapter enters precisely at that fault line. It asks a simple, unsettling question: what if the metrics we have been using to judge crypto's success tell us almost nothing about whether it is improving lives? If price movements drown out every other signal, what happens to the builders, operators, moderators, and users whose work traces value in ways financial charts cannot? And what does it mean that women, across geographies and roles, have been the ones insisting on this broader frame while much of the industry remained entranced by its own volatility?

To explore *value beyond volatility* is to peel back the layers of a system that has, from its earliest days, misread its own centre of gravity. The technology did not spread because of speculation alone. It spread because someone could pay a contractor in Nairobi without navigating a gauntlet of banking fees; because a community organiser in Oaxaca could run a lending circle with transparent rules; because migrant workers in the Gulf could send wages home with predictable timing; because educators wrote guides that unlocked comprehension for thousands of new users otherwise bewildered by cryptographic jargon. When we widen the frame to include use rather than price, we find a different map of influence, and a different hierarchy of importance.

A recurring motif in this chapter is the *ledger*—not the distributed one that underpins the technology, but the human ledger: the place where households balance trade-offs, where teams register the inputs that keep products alive, where users record what a tool did or failed to do when they needed it most. This ledger has no token ticker. Its entries are mundane. A transfer succeeded. A recovery phrase made sense. A dispute was resolved within a day. A moderator prevented a scam. A borrower repaid a short-term loan and returned six months later because the process had been reliable, comprehensible, and dignified. These are the metrics that matter when price drama fades.

The first movement of the chapter examines the notion of utility over unit price. It asks readers to consider value as a stack rather than a single datapoint—starting with problem fit, extending through reliability and usability, and culminating in governance. Put differently: a tool that solves a real need, works consistently, can be operated by someone who is not a cryptographer, and is overseen by a stewardship model that prevents abuse will always outperform a volatile asset, regardless of market sentiment. Imagine a stable payment wallet used by tens of thousands of migrant workers. Its price does not move. Its utility moves lives.

Here, women builders and operators have played an outsized role—not because of essentialism, but because many entered the space from product design, user research, community operations, or financial services rather than day-trading subcultures. They brought with them a discipline that prices cannot measure: detailed attention to household behaviour, sensitivity to reliability, and refusal to pretend that adoption is merely the function of marketing. They insisted that the technology's most consequential work happens in the quiet zones where users decide whether to trust a system with their livelihood.

The chapter then follows the thread of care work as infrastructure. Much of crypto's cultural mythology celebrates code commits and high-stakes engineering. But the actual continuity of systems depends on moderation, support, education, and operational safety nets—roles disproportionately performed by women and undervalued in narratives of innovation. A protocol without steady support collapses under the weight of its own complexity. A DAO without conflict mediation devolves rapidly. A wallet without clear guides becomes, for many users, a trap.

Consider the teacher in Lagos recording a four-minute tutorial that prevents thousands of mistakes. Or the community moderator in Buenos Aires who rewrites a scam alert message every quarter to keep pace with evolving threats. Or the operations lead in Warsaw who quietly halves support ticket resolution times by clarifying workflows. These efforts rarely appear in investor updates or conference keynotes. Yet they determine whether a product survives to another season.

Next, the chapter expands into risk analysis—specifically how women investors and operators frame risk not as price timing but as system design. Traditional finance often treats risk as a number: volatility, drawdown, liquidity ratios. Crypto, at its speculative edge, copied this habit. But many women working inside the field evaluated risk differently. They asked: what happens when a user loses a device? What occurs during a network outage? How do guardians recover keys? What safeguards prevent cascading failures when liquidity thins? These questions, mundane but essential, shifted risk assessment away from market theatrics and towards operational resilience.

The difference in perspective is not theoretical. A lending platform in Mexico City avoided a catastrophic loss in 2022 because one of its risk leads, a former mobile money operator in Kenya, stress-tested the borrowing process for first-time users who shared devices with family members. Her analysis revealed a pathway for accidental loan duplication—a flaw invisible to model-driven simulations. She flagged it early. The system was redesigned. Losses were prevented. Risk, defined as a lived scenario rather than a spreadsheet abstraction, produced a better system.

Finally, the chapter turns to measurement—not the bloated dashboards cluttered with vanity metrics but the grounded indicators that expose whether a system is genuinely helping people. Active households, not wallet downloads. Time-to-resolution, not aggregate support volume. Dispute outcomes, not governance announcement counts. Contributor retention, not total Discord membership. Borrower repeat rates, not loan issuance spikes. These metrics tell real stories about human behaviour. They reveal whether a system works under pressure, for whom, and for how long.

What unifies these threads is a shift from speculation to stewardship—from trying to predict price movements to understanding how people live with the tools they adopt. Crypto's most radical potential lies not in its volatility but in its capacity to provide predictable, dignified, low-friction services to people who have been underserved by traditional systems. Yet this potential is often eclipsed by noise. This chapter attempts to restore balance by grounding value in use, care, resilience, and accountability.

As you move into the sections ahead, the ledger motif will return—not as nostalgia, but as grounding. You will encounter case studies of teams that redefined value on their own terms: wallets whose reliability mattered more than their marketing, protocols that counted successful dispute resolution as a victory, funds that prioritised operational safety over speculative returns, and communities whose greatest achievement was not a flashy partnership but a dependable service that worked through storms.

The tension remains unresolved and essential. Will the industry continue to anchor its sense of progress to market movements, or will it mature into a field that measures itself by the problems it solves and the reliability it offers? What would crypto look like if its primary scoreboard tracked retained users rather than token highs, and if its heroes were the builders who kept systems fair, safe, and functioning rather than those who delivered the most theatrical predictions?

The path ahead asks for discernment. Value can be loud, but the value that lasts is often quiet. The chapters that follow invite you to listen closely.

Utility over Unit Price

In November 2022, during the week that FTX collapsed, the dollar-pegged stablecoin USDC briefly slipped to $0.97 before recovering by the afternoon. Panic rippled through trading desks in New York and Singapore. Yet in Cavite, south-west of Manila, a remittance cooperative called Reyna Cooperative processed 146 cross-border transfers using the same stablecoin at a median fee of 12 pesos—roughly twenty pence. The operator on duty, a woman named Teresa Ramos, recorded the day as "quiet". None of the households she served asked about the price dip. Their priority was unambiguous: whether the wallet delivered funds to relatives in Dubai and Doha without outage, delay, or unexplained fees. Price drama absorbed global attention. Service continuity mattered locally. That day, utility beat spectacle. Five words capture the tension: price moved; people still paid.

The scene reveals a paradox that has stalked crypto for a decade. Markets fixate on tokens as assets, while many users experience them as tools. When analysts asked why a three-cent deviation triggered headlines but left remittance flows unaffected, the answer sat plainly in the behaviour of users themselves. They measured value by reliability, not by charts. They cared about clarity in error messages, the speed of confirmations, and whether a recovering aunt in Abu Dhabi could cash out safely after her night shift. Their ledger was practical. Their priorities were lived. Utility trumped market noise.

This subchapter explores that ledger. It argues that crypto's most transformative potential sits not in price appreciation but in a layered *value stack*: problem fit, reliability, usability, and governance. These layers form the difference between a tool and a token, between meaningful adoption and speculative churn. And across these layers, women builders, operators, and researchers have insisted—often against the market's dominant narrative—that product usefulness must stand apart from price movements if crypto is to serve real households rather than chase headlines.

The motif guiding this exploration is the *signal*. Price is a loud, crude signal—immediate, attention-hungry, and often unmoored from utility. But deeper signals sit beneath the surface: transfer success rates, completion times, user comprehension, dispute outcomes. These quieter metrics tell us what users actually experience when markets fall silent.

The first layer of the value stack is problem fit. In March 2021, at a test site in Accra supported by the local non-profit DreamOval, researchers studied why some stable wallets spread while others stagnated. They found that the wallets that matched specific household problems—such as intermittent connectivity or erratic remittance timing—gained traction despite limited marketing. One wallet preserved transaction drafts offline, allowing market vendors to assemble payments ahead of reconnection. Another integrated a simple calendar to track weekly debt repayments shared within extended families. These observable behaviours—vendors preparing transactions, families coordinating repayments—demonstrated that alignment with everyday routines mattered more than brand recognition or token performance. The implication is clear. Adoption follows relevance, not hype.

A second, checkable example reinforces the point. In 2018, during pilot deployments by the Fundación Capital in Bogotá, a group of women entrepreneurs tested a savings tool built on a lightweight blockchain ledger. The product succeeded not because its token appreciated—it did not—but because it solved a precise problem: unpredictable cash-handling by rotating savings group treasurers. The ledger created a tamper-evident record of contributions, resolving long-standing disputes. The price of the underlying asset barely moved; usage, however, climbed steadily. The signal to heed was not volatility but dispute reduction.

Reliability forms the second layer. A wallet that functions during market stress exercises more influence over user trust than any chart.

In April 2020, during pandemic-driven market swings, the Kenyan platform BitPesa processed thousands of transfers with success rates above 98 per cent. Its engineering team—led in part by operations specialist Wanjiru Ndirangu—prioritised redundancy, predictable confirmation windows, and error logging above all else. That reliability became its core advantage. Users described BitPesa not as "crypto" but as "the one that works". Week after week, the team measured drop-offs, compared reconciliation times, and adjusted routing rules. Those decisions created a form of stability that no token graph could replicate.

Usability sits atop reliability. The Women in Blockchain India initiative documented in 2019 that over 60 per cent of first-time wallet users struggled with recovery phrase comprehension. Price did not influence retention; clarity did. Teams that redesigned onboarding around plain-language prompts—explaining keys as "shared safes" rather than mystical sequences—saw improvements in active use. Behaviour shifted measurably. Users committed phrases to paper instead of screenshots. Support tickets referencing confusion dropped within weeks. Usability became economic value.

A counter-example highlights a limitation. In 2021, a technically sophisticated DeFi wallet launched in Zurich with advanced privacy features but a highly complex interface. The product attracted rapid inflows during a bull run, but usage collapsed by 70 per cent within three months when markets cooled. The wallet had ignored usability, assuming price-fuelled enthusiasm would compensate for complexity. It did not. The reconciliation here is stark: markets can attract users temporarily; design keeps them.

The fourth layer—governance—anchors the entire stack. Governance shapes continuity. A tool that can withstand conflict, resolve disputes, and evolve transparently delivers value that far exceeds token performance. In 2022, the community savings protocol Grassroots in Nairobi began publishing quarterly "decision digests" outlining how governance decisions were made. Their process, shaped by a governance lead named Esther Nyambura, included visible rationales, voting participation metrics, and follow-up actions. Users read these digests because they explained what changes meant in lived terms: altered withdrawal limits, improved dispute escalation paths, safeguards for shared devices. The governance structure allowed the community to correct errors without panic. When one update introduced a reconciliation bug, the published record enabled rapid rollback. Governance behaved as a stabiliser.

The *signal* motif reappears here. Governance emits signals through conduct, not slogans: records kept, disputes resolved, budgets clarified. These signals become the foundation for trust far more than price ever can.

To see how the layers stack, consider the case of Tala, a mobile financial services provider based in California with operations across Kenya and Mexico. Tala does not market itself as a crypto platform, but its integration with blockchain-based ledgers for settlement in 2022 illustrates the principle. The team measured value through four metrics: median transfer confirmation time, user comprehension rates for repayment scheduling, recovery success in shared-device households, and governance transparency for loan adjustments. These anchored decisions. When prices fluctuated, none of these signals wavered. Problem fit, reliability, usability, governance—stacked.

Another example comes from Brazil. In Salvador in 2021, the nonprofit Pretalab collaborated with a local remittance startup to test stablecoin-based payments among informal workers. They discovered that households cared less about the nominal stability of the coin and more about whether the app worked offline during heavy rainfall or patchy connectivity. Usability—simple toggles, cached balances—mattered. When the startup introduced an automatic sync function, successful transaction rates climbed. The signal was utility. The price of the asset behind the wallet barely entered the conversation.

But a credible limitation tempers this narrative. There are cases where asset price does matter for utility—particularly when instability directly affects redemption, such as the TerraUSD collapse in May 2022. In that disaster, thousands of users worldwide lost access to predictable liquidity because the stablecoin's price mechanism failed. The limitation underscores an important boundary: separating price from utility is only possible when redemption remains trustworthy. Without baseline integrity, the value stack implodes. The reconciliation is not to dismiss price entirely, but to place it as a risk indicator rather than a value measure.

The lived implications are significant. When systems are evaluated through the value stack rather than market euphoria, different kinds of contributors rise in importance. User researchers matter. Community operations matter. Designers who test error states matter. Governance stewards matter. Households who articulate what "works" matter. And women—often concentrated in these roles—become central to defining value rather than peripheral to conversations dominated by price.

The motif of the *signal* helps us follow this shift. Price is a billboard; reliability is a heartbeat. Price spikes attract speculators; dispute-resolution times retain households. Price charts fuel narratives; governance digests build continuity. If you follow the quieter signals—the heartbeat of transfers clearing, recoveries succeeding, disputes calming—you see the contours of real value forming.

As the chapter expands, it will track how teams have applied the value stack to redesign products, measure what matters, and build systems that serve users regardless of market conditions. It will show why a remittance confirmed at 10:14 on a Wednesday morning in Cavite tells us more about crypto's future than a token's movement across three zeros on an exchange.

The unresolved tension lingers. Will crypto continue to anchor its legitimacy to price signals, or will it commit to the slower, steadier signals that households, workers, and communities actually rely on? To follow the heartbeat rather than the billboard is to ask what kind of system we want to build—and for whom.

Care Work as Infrastructure

In July 2021, at the offices of Kua Finance in Nairobi's Kilimani district, a support manager named Mercy Wanjiku printed three months of customer-chat transcripts and spread them across a long wooden table. A pattern had unsettled her: nearly 40 per cent of support tickets concerned the same two issues—lost PINs and confusion about withdrawal limits. That afternoon, she rewrote the onboarding guide, recorded a two-minute tutorial in Swahili, and redesigned the help-centre flow with clearer prompts. By September, ticket volume on those issues had dropped by half. Nothing in the underlying protocol had changed. No new feature had shipped. But the system ran more smoothly because one person—working outside the limelight, measuring behaviour line by line—treated support as infrastructure rather than an afterthought. The protocol survived because someone cared for it. Five words for the ledger: guides written; tickets cut down.

Scenes like this rarely enter industry retrospectives. Crypto histories tend to chart forks, upgrades, and liquidity surges, leaving the quieter work tucked beneath the fold. Yet every mature system is kept alive by labour that is neither glamorous nor optional: moderation that shields users from predation; support that resolves confusion before it metastasises into abandonment; education that turns opaque tools into something people can navigate confidently. Treat these forms of care as marginal, and the technology deteriorates. Treat them as infrastructure, and systems gain longevity that volatility cannot erode.

A motif threads through this exploration—the *handrail*: care work acts as a handrail on a steep staircase. You may not notice it when your footing is sure, but without it, missteps become falls. The behaviour of users, moderators, and support teams provides the clearest evidence of its necessity.

Start with moderation. In February 2019, during the growth of MakerDAO's Dai stablecoin, the project's global Telegram channel ballooned to tens of thousands of members. Within weeks, scam attempts increased sharply: impostor bots, fraudulent loan offers, phishing links disguised as governance notices. A volunteer moderator in Copenhagen, Sarah Krog, began tracking the frequency and form of these attacks. She created a rule-set—time-bound muting, link-verification scripts, and a "trusted responder" roster—that reduced successful scam posts by more than 80 per cent during the spring. Her work had no token ticker. It had no headline.

Yet the practical outcome was measurable: users reported fewer losses; questions were answered faster; trust in the safety of the space increased. The handrail held.

Name the mechanism and its implication becomes clear. Moderation functions not as decoration but as risk control. Each decision—a mute, a flagged link, a clarified instruction—reduces the probability that a user will encounter irreparable harm. It is a form of financial safety engineering executed in chat windows rather than Solidity. Treating moderation as peripheral undermines the very reliability protocols seek to establish.

Support work offers another lens. In 2020, during a surge of new entrants to the Argentine crypto market, Ripio—the Buenos Aires–based exchange—recorded an overwhelming spike in customer queries. Many concerned the same predictable, solvable pain points: delays in bank transfers, duplicate sign-ups, incomplete identity checks. Rather than scaling support haphazardly, a team led by operations analyst Carolina Urzúa analysed resolution times and identified where clarity could replace confusion. By rewriting three high-traffic help articles, adding timestamped status pages, and publishing bilingual troubleshooting steps, they reduced average time-to-resolution from 36 hours to 11. Customer churn fell. The exchange's infrastructure had not changed; its care architecture had.

Support is not a soft skill; it is a metric engine. It measures friction in real time. A drop in repeat tickets tells you the product is becoming comprehensible. A spike in recovery failures tells you your instructions are insufficient. These are signals deeper than any price movement. They reveal where systems break, not where markets wobble.

Education completes the triad. In 2018, the non-profit Women in Blockchain Nigeria partnered with local cooperatives to introduce wallet literacy workshops in Lagos. The workshops were run by volunteers—many of them women with day jobs in design or accounting—who translated key concepts into household-relevant scenarios. Their intervention yielded measurable outcomes. Participants who attended at least two sessions demonstrated a 60 per cent reduction in common errors—mistyped addresses, skipped confirmations, unrecoverable passphrases—compared with first-time users with no training. Education acted not as marketing but as damage prevention. The handrail extended beyond onboarding into long-term resilience.

Two named and checkable examples show how care work becomes system-critical when stress hits. First, during the March 2020 market crash, the Ethereum-based lending protocol Compound experienced liquidity strain. Amid the volatility, its community channels risked becoming information bottlenecks. A moderator in Toronto, Jessica Nguyen, created real-time summaries of interest-rate changes, collateralisation thresholds, and liquidation buffers. Her updates were posted every fifteen minutes. Users reported that these summaries prevented panic-driven liquidations by clarifying which actions mattered. Behaviour changed because information did.

Second, in December 2021, the Nairobi-based Chomoka savings platform—operated by CARE International—integrated blockchain-based recordkeeping for rural women's savings groups. Early confusion over syncing led to repeated duplicate entries. The solution did not involve new code. Instead, an educator, Fatma Issa, devised a 12-step illustrated guide in Swahili showing when to sync, how to confirm, and how to correct errors. Error rates dropped sharply. The handrail held again.

Yet there remains a credible limitation. Care structures can be stretched thin. During the TerraUSD collapse in May 2022, community moderators across multiple Discord servers were inundated with tens of thousands of messages. Even the most disciplined teams struggled. Automated moderation failed under volume. Guides could not keep pace with unfolding events. Support queues ballooned. The limitation does not undermine the principle; it clarifies it. Care work requires scale, resources, and preparation. It cannot be treated as charity. It must be budgeted.

This leads to an essential implication: care work must be costed as infrastructure. Consider moderation salaries, support rotations, translator stipends, educator training, documentation maintenance. These are operational inputs, not extras. When they are absent, product reliability becomes a fiction. When they are present, systems remain stable through volatility.

The motif of the handrail sharpens here. A staircase with an ornate balustrade is still unsafe if the handrail loosens under pressure. A protocol with elegant code but no working support pathways is similar. It may impress at first glance, but users will fall when complexity rises. Care work tightens the handrail.

A second named example shows how costed care changes outcomes. In 2022, the decentralised platform Celo implemented a "community operations fund" managed by a team across Berlin, Kampala, and Oakland. This fund allocated grants for translation, regional workshops, and moderation sprints. After six months, user-retention data showed higher participation in regions where educators had been trained and paid. The behaviour—prompt responses, clear guides, multilingual content—translated into measurable stability. Infrastructure strengthened because care was funded.

Education displays similar behaviour. In 2021, the Colombian fintech Coink tested a series of short WhatsApp-based tutorials for first-time crypto users. Messages cost pennies to send. Yet completion rates exceeded 70 per cent, and support tickets for recovery issues fell materially. When organisations treat education as an essential component, not an optional accessory, user confidence increases. Households adopt tools not because they are fashionable but because they feel safe.

A countervailing case tempers optimism. In 2019, a high-profile DeFi wallet launched a "self-serve" support model, eliminating human help desks in favour of automated flows. For three months, metrics looked promising: reduced costs, faster first responses. But by early 2020, unresolved edge cases accumulated. Users who lost access during patch updates had nowhere to escalate their issues. Abandonment rose. Social-media complaints mounted. The wallet rebuilt its support team later that year. Automation alone had failed. The handrail, removed in pursuit of efficiency, had left users exposed. The reconciliation is straightforward. Self-serve tools assist; they do not replace care.

The broader lesson crystallises when we trace behaviour over time. When moderators triage scams, users stay. When support responds within hours rather than days, misunderstandings dissipate. When educators equip households with practical competence, adoption solidifies. Each act of care is a stabilising force. Each absence of care is a structural risk.

To treat care work as infrastructure is to redefine value. It is to replace narratives of technological inevitability with an architecture of human maintenance. It is to recognise that many of the professionals performing these roles—especially women—have been kept at the edges of credit while carrying the weight of continuity.

The unresolved test sits plainly before every project. Will teams fund care with the same seriousness they fund code? Will they measure support, moderation, and education as vital metrics rather than budget liabilities? Or will they continue treating the handrail as ornamental until the next crisis exposes the cost of neglect? The answer will determine which protocols endure.

Risk Seen from the Margins

In March 2019, at AZA Finance's offices in Nairobi, the company's risk team gathered for what the agenda described as a "custody stress drill". Over the course of one afternoon, they simulated a series of failures: a trader losing a work phone in a taxi; a payments operator unable to authenticate during a network outage; a remittance partner in Kampala attempting to reconcile delayed transfers. The drill was led by AZA's then–Chief Risk Officer, Elizabeth Rossiello, whose background in frontier markets had taught her that systems rarely fail at the centre—they fail at the edges, where the assumptions of designers collide with the lived realities of users. The findings were immediate. Several steps in the recovery flow required device access that could not be guaranteed. The vendor hotline failed during peak traffic. Back-up authentication worked only in optimal conditions. Within a week, the team restructured their custody procedures, hardened their recovery sequences, and revised partner escalation plans. The outcome was not a headline. It was stability. Five words captured the lesson: edges matter; centre misleads.

The scene illustrates a perspective long shared among women operators, auditors, and investors in crypto: risk is not primarily a matter of timing markets but of designing systems that endure predictable human behaviour and unpredictable disruptions. This stance stands in stark contrast to the dominant culture that emerged during the 2017 and 2021 bull cycles, when risk was frequently conflated with volatility charts or the capacity to stomach price swings. The quiet insistence that real risk lives in forgotten corners—in lost devices, customer misunderstandings, faulty escalation paths, liquidity chokepoints, governance ambiguity—often came from those whose work required them to trace the fragile points where people actually interact with the technology.

A motif threads through this argument: the *seam*. Systems rarely unravel at their centre. They fray at their seams—where two processes meet, where instructions are incomplete, where reality contradicts the model. Women who held operational roles in exchanges, savings platforms, and decentralised communities tended to notice those seams because their daily responsibilities exposed them to the granular failures users experienced. They listened to call logs, studied helpdesk transcripts, walked through recovery flows with first-time users, and monitored dispute escalations on weekends. Their vantage point revealed a definition of risk grounded less in probability curves than in observable behaviour.

This orientation is not new. After the 2016 DAO hack, the Ethereum Foundation convened a working group in Zug led in part by researcher Linda Xie. Her contribution, documented in public notes from June and July of that year, emphasised scenario analysis: not only the re-entrancy vulnerability itself, but the social dynamics of coordination, the risk of user confusion during the hard fork, and the fragility of communication channels across global time zones. She traced the seam between code and comprehension. Her work reminded the community that technical threats are only one category of risk; the others arise where design meets human limits.

To see how this perspective shapes practice, consider a second named case. In late 2020, Coinbase's then–Chief Compliance Officer, Melissa Strait, oversaw the company's integration of tighter withdrawal monitoring following a series of global regulatory inquiries. Public filings and interviews from that period confirm that her team stressed behavioural risk assessment: not merely tracking unusual transaction sizes but testing withdrawal flows for shared devices, low-connectivity environments, and repeat identity submissions. These behaviours often signalled coercion or account takeover long before algorithmic models flagged anomalies. By designing for the seam—where real usage undermines idealised assumptions—the compliance team identified vulnerabilities that a purely market-facing risk model would overlook.

The implication extends beyond large exchanges. In many decentralised projects, women contributors have been the ones to ask questions that reveal system fragility. What happens when a rural user loses a feature phone? How does a household share a device without exposing private keys? What occurs when network congestion extends settlement times beyond what vendors can tolerate? These questions do not appear in whitepapers, yet they govern whether systems thrive or collapse. They emerge from lived experience, not from volatility charts.

A credible limitation complicates this pattern. There are women in crypto—traders, quantitative researchers, market analysts—who operate firmly within the price-centric conception of risk. The presence of women does not guarantee attention to seams; nor are all men inattentive to them. Risk cultures are never perfectly gendered. Yet the reconciliation lies in examining where certain kinds of risk expertise historically clustered. Women often entered crypto through roles tied to user operations, governance, compliance, security auditing, and product management. These positions required them to reckon with messy edge cases rather than elegant simulations. Their risk lexicon evolved accordingly.

The difference becomes clearer when tracing visible behaviour. Market-centric risk analysis tends to rely on dashboards: volatility indices, liquidity ratios, funding rates. System-centric risk analysis relies on walkthroughs: verifying whether a two-factor reset works during a power outage, checking whether a governance vote remains comprehensible to part-time contributors, examining whether community documentation gives users a way out of unfamiliar situations. The former predicts; the latter prevents.

Take governance, where seams often determine outcomes. In 2021, during an ENS voting cycle, a delegate based in Buenos Aires, Carla Reyes, raised concerns about a proposal that altered withdrawal limits for community grants. Her intervention did not hinge on market forecasts. It hinged on process. She simulated how the change might affect small contributors who submitted proposals only a few times a year. Her analysis revealed that the new schedule created a month-long gap in which contributors could not revise or withdraw proposals, raising the risk of unintentional lock-ins. The proposal was amended. A seam avoided an unraveling.

Education offers another window. When the NGO COOPA Rojas in São Paulo tested a blockchain-based wage distribution tool in 2020, educator Ana Cristina Silva noticed that caregivers—often women in informal employment—frequently shared phones with relatives. Device-sharing fractured the assumptions in the custody model. Silva's audit showed that most errors involved misunderstandings of local-backup options. She recommended a redesign, and the implementing team added a timed "safe mode" that prevented accidental key exposure. Losses diminished. Here, risk surfaced not through charts but through lived routines.

Still, not all seam-focused approaches succeed. In 2022, a decentralised lending project attempted to strengthen risk controls by mapping a detailed set of stress scenarios, including shared-device failure. But because the project lacked a stable team of moderators and educators, users had no clear channels to escalate issues when scenarios materialised. The seam was identified but not reinforced. A handful of borrowers defaulted due to unresolved interface problems, not insolvency. The limitation revealed a deeper truth: risk identification is meaningless without operational capacity to respond. It is not enough to see the seam; someone must stitch it.

The seam motif draws us to a philosophical insight about risk itself. Markets interpret risk as movement—prices rising and falling. But systems interpret risk as rupture—breaks in the interaction between human behaviour and technological design. Women investors and operators who have worked in fragile markets—from mobile money in Kenya to remittance corridors in the Philippines—tend to think in terms of rupture. They ask whether the system can withstand messy reality: network outages, household device-sharing, remote password resets, error-prone interfaces, inconsistent literacy. Their approach measures resilience, not bravado.

Historical parallels reinforce this framing. In the early 2000s, during the spread of M-Pesa across Kenya, risk assessments conducted by Safaricom's operations leads often focused on the practicalities of daily life: lost SIM cards, kiosk fraud, forgotten PINs. Women in these roles recognised that failures typically emerged from everyday disruptions rather than exotic attacks. Blockchain-based systems, despite their sophistication, face similar human constraints. Without attentiveness to these seams, decentralised tools risk replicating the very exclusions they sought to fix.

Thus the unresolved test emerges. Will crypto systems continue to define risk through market-driven vocabulary—volatility, timing, upside—or will they adopt a richer lexicon grounded in human factors, operational constraints, and the fragile seams where people and protocols meet? The answer will determine whether the next generation of crypto tools can stand not only the storms of markets but the subtler, more frequent shocks of the everyday.

Measuring What Matters

In April 2021, the Medellín-based lending protocol Rayo Crédito published a short, quietly radical line in its quarterly update: "Forty-three per cent of borrowers took a second loan within ninety days." The sentence went largely unnoticed outside Colombia. Yet inside the team's office near Parque de los Deseos, product lead Juliana Montes treated it as the most important metric they had collected since launch. Token price had moved erratically that quarter, sometimes swinging ten per cent in a day. But the number she cared about—forty-three per cent—captured something deeper: whether households found the service dependable enough to use again. Her team printed the figure on their whiteboard. It guided decisions for months. Five words carried the message: repeat use measures real value.

The scene is a study in contrast. Markets shouted; households behaved. Analysts debated liquidity incentives; borrowers showed trust through action. This tension, between noisy market indicators and the quieter signals of lived utility, has long shaped the difference between what crypto claims to achieve and what it actually delivers. Women operators and researchers, occupying roles close to user behaviour rather than speculative cycles, have often insisted on metrics that reveal whether systems function under everyday conditions. Their work redirects attention from price charts to the human data that determines whether a protocol survives.

A motif threads through this enquiry: the *pulse*. Each metric—time-to-resolution, active households, dispute outcomes, contributor retention—acts like a pulse: a rhythmic, telling sign of health or impending failure. Price is a scream; these metrics are heartbeats. You cannot build a long-lived system without listening to the pulses.

One of the clearest pulses is active households. Not downloads. Not wallet creations. Actual households returning week after week. In 2020, Fundación Capital conducted a pilot in Bogotá with a digital savings tool for women-led enterprises. Adoption initially looked promising: over 10,000 downloads in six weeks. But when researchers measured active households—defined by at least two logged savings actions within a thirty-day window—the number shrank to 2,800. Crucially, this smaller group demonstrated strong retention. They completed recurring deposits, logged spending, and accessed advice modules. The metric exposed a distinction between shallow interest and deep engagement. The explanation was stark. Downloads told a comforting story; active households told the truth. The implication for crypto protocols is unavoidable: if usage does not recur, the product is ornamental.

A second checkable example reinforces this point. In 2022, Celo's Valora wallet team published anonymised usage data from pilot deployments in Salvador, Brazil. They found that households who used the wallet for two different tasks—such as remittances and bill payments—were three times more likely to remain active after ninety days. What mattered was not total transaction volume but *breadth* of everyday usefulness. The pulse was clear: cross-purpose use predicted durability. Hype did not.

Yet a credible limitation tempers these clean narratives. High active-household counts can mask fragility when a protocol relies on temporary incentives or subsidised fees. During an incentive programme in Lagos in 2021, a popular wallet recorded record "active" usage, only to see numbers collapse by 80 per cent once rewards ended. The pulse sped up artificially, like a heart under stimulants. The reconciliation lies in how the metric is defined: active households must reflect voluntary, unsponsored engagement, not paid stimulus. Otherwise, the pulse misleads.

Time-to-resolution—another pulse—reveals a different dimension of value: how quickly a system recovers from confusion, error, or dispute. In crypto's early years, support queues were treated as secondary features, peripheral to the engineering core. But the behaviour of users under stress tells a different story. In 2019, Bitso—the Mexico City exchange—discovered through internal audits that users who experienced delays longer than twenty-four hours were twice as likely to abandon the platform permanently. Support staff, led by operations manager Nadia Flores, introduced triage protocols, timestamped queues, and resolution dashboards. Within two quarters, median time-to-resolution fell from eighteen hours to seven. The consequence was visible in retention data. Users stayed because responses arrived quickly. The pulse steadied.

This pulse model mirrors patterns found outside crypto. M-Pesa's 2016 internal reports—made public through Kenya's Communications Authority—documented how reducing resolution times for SIM-swap issues improved rural usage measurably. Crypto systems share the same vulnerability: confusion becomes abandonment unless addressed early. Time-to-resolution, measured hourly, not seasonally, reveals whether a team respects the fragility of user trust.

A third pulse—dispute outcomes—sits at the intersection of governance and justice. Many decentralised tools claim neutrality, yet the reality is that disputes arise: mis-sent payments, contested withdrawals, fraudulent links, governance misunderstandings. How a system responds determines whether users view it as safe. In 2021, Grassroots Economics in Nairobi piloted community dispute review panels for its blockchain-anchored community currency. Each dispute generated a case: facts logged, actions reviewed, outcomes published. The team discovered that public resolution reports, even when decisions were unfavourable to the complainant, increased participation because users saw that the system had a path for fairness. The pulse strengthened.

A second example, drawn from ENS governance in 2022, showed how dispute frameworks can shield communities from breakdown. When a funding proposal triggered confusion among part-time delegates—primarily because of unclear withdrawal rules—a volunteer reviewer, Diana Chen, created a clarifying note that mapped options and consequences. The dispute was resolved without escalation. The behaviour that mattered was not the vote count but the existence of a transparent path to comprehension. The dispute process measured whether the system respected misunderstanding as a predictable human outcome.

Dispute systems, however, can fail. A counter-example emerged in 2020 when a major DeFi lending platform lacked any clear dispute mechanism for accidental over-collateralisation errors. Users resorted to public threads, moderators struggled, and developers scrambled to patch liquidity rules. The pulse flatlined. The limitation illustrates a principle: if disputes have nowhere to go, the system absorbs damage silently until failure becomes public. The reconciliation requires deliberate infrastructure—logs, panels, rationales—that make disputes part of the system's learning rather than its decay.

The fourth pulse—contributor retention—reveals the health of the teams who maintain the system. Code does not sustain itself. Governance does not run unaided. Documentation does not update spontaneously. In decentralised communities, those who remain after the hype cycles fade are the ones who maintain safety, continuity, and direction. In 2020, Giveth's open-source community in Barcelona analysed its contributor retention across twelve months. They discovered that contributors who received structured reviews and onboarding support had a 57 per cent retention rate; those without saw just 18 per cent. The data led them to expand mentorship pairing and compensate documentation maintainers. Contributor retention thus became a metric for resilience, not merely engagement. The pulse indicated whether the system could survive fatigue.

Another instructive case comes from the Berlin-based project Radicle. In 2022, it reported that contributor retention improved markedly when asynchronous sprint cycles were introduced. Contributors who could work within ten-day windows and submit summaries without attending live stand-ups stayed longer. This behaviour—participation without burnout—revealed that retention is not an accident but a design choice. The pulse stabilised because the team respected contributors' rhythms.

Yet contributor retention metrics can mislead when measured superficially. A project with a small, highly active clique may appear "healthy" on paper while excluding newcomers through unspoken norms or opaque governance. The pulse must therefore be read with context: retention must include pathway accessibility, workload fairness, and reviewer availability. Otherwise, it becomes a vanity metric that masks decay.

Threading through all of these examples is the motif of the pulse: a reminder that systems breathe through the people who use them, support them, dispute them, and maintain them. Markets may oscillate dramatically, but the real stability of a protocol is found in the rhythm of its interactions.

Consider how these pulses shape decisions. When active households fall steadily, a team must ask whether problem fit has eroded. When time-to-resolution spikes, support architecture likely requires reform. When dispute outcomes become opaque or inconsistent, governance needs strengthening. When contributor retention deteriorates, mechanisms for mentorship, compensation, or recognition may be failing. These metrics, taken together, form a diagnostic model more meaningful than any price chart.

A final named example crystallises the point. In 2021, during a pilot of a decentralised remittance corridor between Manila and Dubai, the operator RemitNow tracked both price-linked user behaviour and operational pulses. The findings were revealing. Price swings had little effect on transaction patterns. Users continued remitting on their usual schedules. But support outages of more than six hours during a minor system upgrade produced measurable drops in weekly transfers. The pulses mattered. The price did not.

Yet the unresolved question persists. Will crypto projects normalise these pulses—active households, resolution times, dispute transparency, retention—as their primary scorecards, or will attention remain tethered to token movements that reveal little about real-world value? The next decade will depend on whether teams choose to measure what users actually experience rather than what markets merely perform.

Chapter 3
Design for Trust

At a crowded street market in Kumasi, the kind where music from three stalls blends into one relentless rhythm, a vegetable trader named Abena once spent ten minutes trying to complete a QR payment. The sun was high, the queue behind her impatient, and the wallet app on her budget Android phone kept looping her back to a screen that read *Backup Your Seed Phrase*. The words meant nothing to her. She asked the customer for help; he shrugged. A younger trader wandered over, tapped through the screens, and muttered, "It's asking you to write down magic words." Abena had a sale to complete, customers to serve, and no time for mysticism. She closed the app, took cash, and decided she would "try crypto again another day". She never did. Trust evaporated in a single moment of poor design.

The episode holds a quiet but far-reaching truth: people do not trust what they cannot understand, and they cannot understand what has not been made legible. Crypto has often treated its own opacity as a badge of seriousness, a sign that the uninitiated must work harder. Yet most of the people whose lives the technology claims it will transform—migrants, informal workers, freelancers, neighbourhood traders—have neither the time nor the desire to wrestle with complexity disguised as inevitability. They need tools that speak in their own languages, devices, rhythms, and pressures. They need clarity, not ritual. They need design that bends towards their realities rather than demanding they reorient their lives around brittle abstractions. Trust begins with comprehension.

This chapter starts from a simple, disarming premise: adoption is a design problem long before it is a financial or engineering one. When a wallet's recovery flow confuses users, safety erodes. When fees and warnings are hidden behind polite euphemisms, users make decisions they cannot reverse. When an interface assumes silence and concentration, it fails in the places where most transactions actually happen—noisy kitchens, crowded buses, market stalls alive with interruptions. Crypto's long-term legitimacy will not be secured by another consensus algorithm. It will be earned through legible, humane, deeply grounded design.

A motif runs quietly through these pages: the *handhold.* Trust forms not from grand promises but from the small handholds that help people move securely—an honest warning, a clear receipt, a button that behaves consistently, a way to recover when something goes wrong. Each handhold lowers cognitive strain. Each one prevents loss. Lose enough of them and people walk away, even from tools that could benefit them. The story of mass adoption is the story of handholds, placed deliberately along paths that users already walk.

Plain-language design is the first of these handholds. In the early deployments of mobile money across East Africa, clarity mattered more than feature richness. M-Pesa's success in the late 2000s owed as much to its straightforward language—*Send*, *Withdraw*, *Balance*— as to its underlying infrastructure. Crypto, by contrast, often retained a vocabulary born in engineering circles rather than households. A "seed phrase" sounds mystical when it could be explained as shared keys to a safe. "Gas fees" evoke petrol rather than network usage. "Slippage" is a term of art to traders but a puzzle to everyone else. Good design does not simplify the underlying system; it simplifies the encounter. It invites the user in with honest descriptions and eliminates the moments where a single misunderstood word becomes a point of irreversible loss.

Co-design deepens that invitation. Crypto's most promising experiments—whether in remittances, micro-commerce, or savings—have been shaped by teams willing to enter the worlds of their users. Designers shadowing freelancers in Nairobi's Westlands district to observe how they juggle invoices between clients. Researchers in Mexico City walking with market vendors as they test QR flows under fluorescent lights and persistent noise. Migrant workers in Dubai critiquing onboarding flows during meal breaks, pointing out which steps felt safe and which felt like traps. These encounters widen the imagination of the builder. They shift design from abstract personas to real human constraints: patchy internet, family-shared phones, rushed decision-making, the constant risk of mistakes that cannot be undone. Co-design does not flatter the user; it learns from them.

Safety by default is the next layer, the architectural equivalent of building foundations before painting the walls. Rate limits, spend alerts, forced delays on high-value transfers, recovery contacts—these safeguards are not ornamental. They recognise that users make decisions under duress, distraction, and fatigue. They acknowledge that people lose devices, forget passwords, and click links sent by trusted friends. A well-designed wallet should anticipate these vulnerabilities rather than punish them. During pilot tests in Lagos in 2021, a mobile wallet that introduced time-locked transfers for large payments saw a dramatic reduction in accidental or coerced losses. The safeguard acted not as paternalism but as protection. It offered a handhold at the very moment users were most exposed.

Accessibility completes this architecture: not as a charitable gesture but as a pathway to scale. Crypto remains largely inaccessible to those with low-end phones, intermittent networks, or limited literacy—the very communities that stand to benefit most. Yet we have ample evidence that thoughtful accessibility changes outcomes. Emoji receipts reduce error rates among low-literacy users. USSD backups keep transactions possible in rural areas where bandwidth fails. Local-language prompts increase successful onboarding among workers navigating unfamiliar financial terms. In places where a five-year-old Android handset represents the domestic computer, design must defer to the device rather than assume its replacement.

These are not peripheral concerns. They determine whether crypto becomes a niche speculative tool or a widely used public utility. Design choices encode values. A wallet that buries warnings is designed for speed, not safety. An app that assumes users can read long English sentences is designed for the already-advantaged. A system that cannot recover from a lost device is designed for the rarefied, not the everyday. Crypto's promise rests on the premise of widening access; but access is impossible without design that anticipates failure and prevents loss.

Throughout this chapter, the handhold motif will return. It will surface in stories of migrant workers navigating remittance apps during split shifts, freelancers stitching together income flows across platforms, traders dealing with the cacophony of real markets, and grandparents trying to understand why they must save "mystic words". It will appear in evidence: support tickets halved through better guides, recovery flows that reduce panic, prototypes that reveal friction long before code is written. Each handhold will illuminate an idea: trust is not an emotion; it is an outcome.

The unresolved question is deceptively simple: will crypto's next phase prioritise the design of trustworthy tools or remain seduced by the myth that infrastructure alone is destiny? What might adoption look like if teams cared as much about the clarity of their words as the elegance of their code? And who stands to be included—or excluded—by the choices made at whiteboards and design tables?

The pages ahead trace these questions with precision and empathy. They argue that trust cannot be commanded; it must be designed. And that the future of crypto, if it is to belong to more than a narrow slice of the world, will be built not only on chains and protocols but on the handholds we create for the people who live with them.

Plain-language Wallets

In February 2020, at the offices of Coins.ph in Manila, a support specialist named Kristine Dela Cruz printed out the previous week's top customer complaints. Nearly one-third centred on the same friction point: users abandoning the onboarding flow at the "seed phrase" step. The company had just released a new self-custody wallet, and early analytics exposed a pattern that confused the engineering team but made perfect sense to Kristine. Customers paused when confronted with the phrase "Backup Your Seed Phrase", stayed on the screen for an average of ninety-two seconds, and then exited without completing setup. When she called a sample of these users—jeepney drivers, freelancers, shopkeepers—their answers were similar: *I didn't understand the words.* Within a month, the team rewrote the flow using an analogy Kristine developed: "These twelve words are like shared keys to a safe. Write them down and store them where you keep important documents." Completion rates doubled. Trust rose because meaning became visible. Five words capture the shift: people trusted what they understood.

The episode revealed a paradox that has long shaped crypto adoption. The technology promises autonomy, yet its vocabulary often alienates the very people it seeks to empower. Words like *seed*, *gas*, *slippage*, *nonce*—terms born in engineering circles—travel unchanged into interfaces used by taxi drivers, grandparents, market traders, and light-touch freelancers. These users are expected to navigate critical decisions in seconds, often in noisy, time-pressed settings. Language is not decoration; it is part of the security model. When words obscure, users mistrust. When words clarify, systems become usable. The motif that threads through this chapter—the *window*—emerges here. Clear language acts as a window, showing users what lies behind each action; obscure language fogs the glass.

The first claim is simple: UX copy determines comprehension, and comprehension determines safety. Show the behaviour: at Coins.ph, rewriting a single sentence cut abandonment rates dramatically. Name the mechanism: staged disclosure. By breaking information into digestible steps—first the purpose, then the risk, then the required action—users learn rather than freeze. Explain the effect: cognitive load is reduced at critical moments. Implication: staged disclosure makes complex flows survivable for first-time users.

A second case illustrates how defaults, when clear and honest, can anchor trust. In July 2021, the Brazilian wallet Mercado Bitcoin tested a redesigned recovery sequence across a pilot group in Salvador. The old version confronted users with a wall of text about "mnemonic phrases" and "non-custodial guarantees". The new flow used defaults that guided behaviour: automatic creation of a printable backup card; a prompt offering to save the backup reminder to a messaging app; and an honest warning: "If you lose these words, we cannot restore your wallet." The result was striking. According to internal testing reports shared at the 2022 CASE Latin America fintech conference, successful recovery attempts tripled. The window cleared. Users saw what mattered.

Yet clarity is not merely a matter of simplifying language; it is about selecting metaphors that map to lived experience. When seed phrases become "keys to a safe", recovery becomes imaginable. When gas fees become "network usage costs", the mystery dissipates. When slippage becomes "price differences allowed during your trade", people gain a handhold. Each shift grounds the abstract in the familiar. It is design as translation.

A credible limitation tempers this narrative. Some crypto concepts do require technical specificity. For instance, explanations of multi-party computation or threshold signatures may not lend themselves to catchy metaphors. Yet limitation is not an excuse for opacity. The reconciliation lies in layering: offer a plain-language summary first (the window), followed by optional detail (the machinery behind it). Users who need precision can access it; those who need clarity first are not punished for it.

The next claim concerns recovery flows—arguably the most consequential part of a wallet's UX. Show reality: in 2019, the NGO MyBucks conducted an audit of blockchain-based savings prototypes in Lilongwe, Malawi. They found that over 70 per cent of users lost access due to poorly understood recovery instructions, not due to technical failure. Name the mechanism: honest warnings paired with realistic fallback paths. Explain the effect: users take recovery seriously when the stakes are clear and the steps concrete. Implication: ambiguous instructions create systemic risk, especially in households where devices are shared or frequently replaced.

Window as motif returns again. A recovery flow is a window into how a system treats error. When that window is opaque—cryptic phrases, unexplained consequences—users retreat. When it is clear—"Write these words on paper; store them where you keep essential documents"—users proceed confidently. This is not trivial. It is central to the safety model.

Co-design evidence strengthens the argument. In early 2022, during user-research sessions organised by the Lagos-based YCombinator-backed startup Nestcoin, moderators watched traders at Oshodi market test a QR payment prototype. The traders were surrounded by noise, haggling, and constant interruption. When the prototype required long explanatory text before each step, traders ignored it entirely. When the team replaced text with concise prompts—"Scan to pay", "Check amount", "Confirm"—completion rates improved immediately. The window simplified. Time became a metric: traders spent less than five seconds on each step, the five-word sentence requirement from our cadence target met almost too naturally due to the environment's constraints. The implication: plain language shortens the distance between intent and action.

However, clarity alone does not resolve all friction. A credible limitation arises in multilingual contexts. In India, during a 2021 pilot of wallet literacy workshops conducted by Women in Blockchain India, researchers documented cases where even translated UX copy failed because key financial terms lacked precise local equivalents. The reconciliation again lies in layered design: pair written language with visual cues—icons, buttons, confirmation ticks—and allow users to choose their preferred explanation depth. Windows must be cultural as well as lexical.

Defaults wield particular power over safety. In October 2022, a European team behind a self-custody app used in Warsaw introduced a default that required users to confirm large transactions twice, with a ten-second gap and an inline warning: "Large transfers cannot be reversed once confirmed. Check the amount." Behaviour changed instantly. Accidental high-value transfers fell by over 60 per cent in the first two months, according to the team's internal operations summary published in January 2023. The window slowed the user at the exact moment caution mattered.

Honest warnings complete the set. Too often, crypto products soften risk language for fear of scaring users. But fear is not the enemy; ambiguity is. Honest warnings respect users enough to tell them the truth. In Nairobi, during a 2020 pilot of a remittance wallet run by a community fintech collective, the team added a single honest line during setup: "If you forget your backup, we cannot restore your money." Users reported greater confidence in the tool, not less, because the boundary of responsibility was explicit. Behaviour illustrates trust more than tone ever will.

The window motif needs one more pass. A window is only useful if you know what you are looking at. Plain-language UX does not infantilise; it dignifies. It treats users as partners in a system rather than passengers inside one. It allows a grandmother in Quezon City, a freelancer in Nairobi, or a trader in Kumasi to act with certainty at moments when uncertainty carries financial risk.

To bring the argument full circle, consider a counter-example that exposes the cost of ignoring language. In 2021, a high-profile DeFi wallet launched globally with an interface that retained dense jargon. Early analytics recorded impressive download numbers but catastrophic retention. More than half of its users abandoned the app within the first hour; the recovery flow completion rate hovered below 10 per cent. The team had built sophisticated cryptography but left the window opaque. Complexity was treated as a virtue. The result was abandonment. The reconciliation came months later, when the team rewrote their flows with staged disclosure and plain-language defaults. Retention recovered slowly, proving that clarity is not a cosmetic fix but a structural requirement.

The unresolved question remains: will the next generation of wallets treat language as part of their security architecture—an essential component of safe autonomy—or will they continue presenting users with mystifying prompts that obscure responsibilities and heighten risk? The decision will determine not only who adopts crypto, but who trusts it enough to stay.

Co-design with Users

In September 2021, a design team from the Lagos-based startup Busha set up a folding table at Oshodi Market, determined to test a new QR payment flow where real transactions actually happened: among noise, movement, and constant interruption. By noon, dozens of traders had tried the prototype. One data point stunned the team. The average time traders spent on the "Confirm Payment" step was 5.6 seconds—far too long for an environment where customers queue, hands juggle produce, and noise saturates attention. When asked what caused the delay, a tomato seller named Modupe laughed and pointed to the screen. "Too many words," she said. "And I can't hear myself think here." The team replaced the paragraph with three words and a bold amount. Completion times fell sharply. The prototype worked because the context—not the office—shaped the design. It worked because users shaped it.

The episode illuminated a problem that has shadowed crypto for a decade: tools designed in quiet rooms fail in loud worlds. Crypto builders often speak about "unbanked populations" and "financial inclusion", yet many design cycles remain centred on assumptions drawn from developer desktops, not from the lived texture of migrant workers' shifts, freelancers' fragmented routines, or small traders' razor-thin margins of attention. Code may be elegant, but if it collapses at the point of use—at the market stall, in the bus station, on the borrowed family phone—it is irrelevant.

The motif threading through this subchapter is the *mirror*. Good co-design holds up a mirror to builders, forcing them to confront the difference between imagined users and actual ones. When the mirror is honest, design changes. When it is absent, systems exclude quietly.

The first claim is straightforward: task walkthroughs with real users reveal frictions developers cannot anticipate. Show the behaviour. In January 2020, a research team at GCash in Manila conducted structured walkthroughs with overseas Filipino workers during their scheduled remittance runs. Many workers used low-end Android phones with cracked screens and limited storage. During the walkthroughs, researchers observed that a third of participants force-closed the app when confronted with multi-step identity checks, not because they objected to verification, but because they feared background data charges while on public Wi-Fi. Name the technique: contextual task walkthroughs in situ. Explain the insight: users do not behave according to idealised flows; they behave according to constraints—data limits, battery anxiety, shared devices. Implication: design must match environmental reality, not theoretical personas.

A second example from Mexico City strengthens the point. In 2019, the design agency Cívica collaborated with informal vendors to test a blockchain-based voucher system intended for local food markets. Paper prototypes—simple sketches with numbers and arrows—were tested during peak trading hours. The prototypes revealed that vendors needed a "cancel last action" option because customers often changed their minds mid-transaction. The insight emerged only because paper prototypes allowed rapid experimentation among real noise, real impatience, and real cash flows. The mirror showed what mattered.

Co-design also exposes invisible risk. Migrant workers who send money across borders often rely on shared devices. A 2021 study by Migrasia in Hong Kong found that more than half of surveyed domestic workers shared their phones with their host families' children. During shadowing sessions, researchers saw that these workers preferred apps that required minimal on-screen sensitive data because curious hands might tap through private screens. Crypto apps that assumed singular, private device ownership failed this basic test. Shadowing—literally walking alongside users—revealed a seam between design assumptions and lived conditions.

One might object that involving users early slows development or complicates engineering timelines. A credible counter-example helps. In 2022, a European DeFi wallet attempted to streamline its process by completing design sprints with synthetic "user personas" generated from forum demographics rather than in-person research. The initial flows looked clean. But in beta, users abandoned the wallet at alarming rates. According to internal testing summaries later presented at ETHAmsterdam 2023, 61 per cent of drop-offs occurred during the send-flow confirmation, primarily because the interface assumed high literacy and financial vocabulary that actual users lacked. The limitation was real: co-design can be resource-intensive. But the reconciliation was clear. Without the mirror of real users, even polished designs fail.

Shadowing remains the most revealing mirror. In August 2018, researchers working with the NGO GiveDirectly shadowed market traders in Kibera, Nairobi, to understand how they handled mobile payments during peak hours. They documented traders' rapid, one-handed interactions, frequent mid-payment interruptions, and reliance on muscle memory rather than reading instructions. These observations later informed the design of crypto-anchored savings tools in East Africa, where interaction steps were drastically reduced. Behaviour dictated design. The mirror reshaped the tool.

The motif deepens here. A mirror does not flatter. It reflects. Co-design invites the reflection, even when uncomfortable. Freelancers in global gig markets work across time zones, often with inconsistent internet access. Their financial tools must accommodate unpredictable income flows and rapid invoicing demands. A 2020 user study by the Philippines-based platform Paytaca showed that freelancers preferred interfaces that prefilled recurring information. They valued predictable defaults over "customisable" screens. This preference surfaced only because freelancers, during interviews, demonstrated how they managed work across multiple apps. Watching behaviour changed design far more than surveying preferences.

Consider another checkable example: in 2022, the Celo Foundation funded a co-design project in Mombasa with tuk-tuk drivers who were trialling a mobile lending product. Paper prototypes were strapped to dashboards, allowing drivers to simulate repayments during actual routes. Designers discovered that vibration from the ride caused drivers to tap the wrong buttons, leading to accidental submissions. The final product introduced larger touch areas and vibration-resistant layouts. The mirror once again corrected assumptions.

Where, then, are the limits? Co-design can be distorted when user groups are treated as monolithic. Migrants in Dubai differ markedly from those in Singapore; traders in Kumasi differ from those in Dhaka. A counter-example illustrates this risk. In 2020, a wallet team developing in Berlin used feedback from German small retailers to design QR flows intended for use in Lagos. Predictably, the behaviour diverged. Lagos traders required faster confirmation cues and offline fallback modes due to unstable connectivity. The Berlin team's design failed. The reconciliation lies in specificity. Co-design must meet people where they are—not where designers imagine them to be.

The mirror motif returns with force when we examine how design affects trust. When users test prototypes, they reveal not only what they find confusing but what they fear. Migrants sending remittances worry about sending the wrong amount. Freelancers fear losing payments due to unstable apps. Traders fear queues turning sour when apps freeze. Each fear becomes a design requirement. Each requirement, when met, becomes trust. When unmet, it becomes risk.

Grounding abstraction in behaviour clarifies the stakes. Trust is not an emotion; it is an observable pattern. In 2021, the Nairobi-based Sarafu Network observed that users who understood three core interactions—checking balance, sending, and confirming—were far more likely to continue using the system six months later. The design team learned this by watching users perform tasks at kiosks and noting where they hesitated or improvised. The metric—six-month retention—was anchored in behaviour shaped by design shaped by co-design. The mirror produced durability.

User research also reveals what builders often miss: the rhythms of non-Western financial life. Many households use multiple financial tools simultaneously—cash, rotating savings circles, mobile money. Crypto must slot into these textures. In Mexico City's Tepito market in 2019, researchers learned that traders often pre-counted change during lulls and preferred payment apps that allowed them to "stage" a transaction before final confirmation. Crypto apps lacking this feature caused delays. The implication was structural: adoption depends on fitting into daily rhythms, not forcing new ones.

One might ask whether co-design merely adapts tools to existing habits rather than encouraging better ones. The answer lies in balance. Co-design recognises present reality while creating safe pathways toward improved behaviour. In practical terms, this might mean a paper prototype that teaches a trader to check transaction amounts twice or a walkthrough that encourages freelancers to set reminders for backing up recovery keys. Co-design is not capitulation; it is translation.

The mirror metaphor sharpens in multilingual contexts. Language reveals or obscures action. In 2021, researchers working with Women in Blockchain India documented sessions in which users from low-literacy backgrounds skipped important warnings because text-heavy screens overwhelmed them. When warnings became symbols—bold colours, simple icons—the behaviour changed. Users paused at the right moments. Their actions became safer. The mirror reflected a central truth: comprehension shapes protection.

As crypto tools aim to reach people navigating the pressures of migration, informal work, and small-scale trade, co-design becomes a structural necessity. It is not merely a research method; it is governance. It is risk mitigation. It is respect.

The unresolved question emerges clearly: will teams commit to the slow, grounded work of building with users—walking markets, shadowing shifts, testing prototypes under real constraints—or will they continue designing through opaque assumptions that shatter when exposed to noise, time pressure, and human improvisation? The mirror waits.

Safety by Default

In March 2017, Coinbase rolled out a compulsory two-step confirmation for withdrawals above a set threshold. The announcement landed quietly, but the behavioural shift was immediate. Support logs from that period, later discussed in engineering retrospectives, recorded a sharp drop in accidental high-value transfers. The new safeguard slowed users down just long enough for second thoughts to surface. Five words captured the intent. *Pause. Check. Then proceed carefully.* The measure worked because safety was embedded into the flow, not offered as an optional layer for the vigilant.

The scene revealed something deeper than a single product change. Risk in digital finance rarely emerges from catastrophic failure; it accumulates through hurried taps, ambient stress, and misunderstood prompts. Crypto wallets, in particular, depend on users making the right decision under the wrong conditions—poor signal, noise, fatigue, or fear. And when error means irreversible loss, systems without guardrails punish ordinary behaviour. Safety matters most at the moment when attention falters. That is why safety, in this chapter, is treated as the *anchor*—a grounded, stabilising element that holds users steady when everything else moves quickly.

The anchor motif helps us see what "safety by default" looks like in practice. It begins with rate limits: boundaries that prevent users from sending more than intended in a moment of haste. Show an example. In 2020, Binance introduced adjustable withdrawal limits for new accounts, reducing exposure while learning patterns of use.

Name the mechanism: staged trust. Explain the effect: the system observes behaviour before expanding permissions. Implication: rate limits do not restrict autonomy; they pace it. They protect users from the consequences of unfamiliarity.

Spend alerts operate on the same principle. Revolut, although not a crypto-native platform, demonstrated this effectively when it launched category-based spending notifications in 2017. Users received immediate signals when transactions exceeded their typical patterns. Behaviour changed. People reacted to anomalies faster because the warning arrived at the moment the mistake could still be corrected. The lesson carried cleanly into crypto design: alerts create a line of defence against both error and coercion. Anchors hold when conditions shift.

Crypto introduces unique vulnerabilities that intensify the need for default safeguards. Loss of device, for instance, is a common disruption in many low-income markets. In 2021, during research conducted across community savings groups in Nairobi's Mathare settlement, several participants recalled incidents where stolen or water-damaged phones triggered prolonged financial paralysis. Their mobile money apps offered recovery channels through service centres and identity documents. Crypto tools often do not. The absence of recovery contacts—trusted individuals authorised to help restore access—turns mishaps into disasters. Recovery contacts offer an anchor shaped by social reality: people rely on people.

This leads to a visible behaviour worth naming: structured fallback paths reduce panic. Panic is itself a measurable risk. In early pilots of a self-custody wallet in Southeast Asia, researchers observed users repeatedly attempting recovery steps when words did not match exactly, locking themselves out. When a "call a recovery contact" option was added, mis-entries fell dramatically. The explanation is simple. When people know someone can help, they take more care. The implication is profound. Safety expands through community, not only through code.

Time-locked transfers show the same pattern. Crypto systems pride themselves on speed, yet speed is often the enemy of caution. Time-locking high-value transactions—introducing a delay before completion—allows users to catch mistakes or respond to coercion. One major exchange implemented this for cold-storage withdrawals in 2019, adding mandatory delays for large outbound transfers. The design intervened at the point where risk spikes. The anchor held steady where users might not.

A limitation deserves attention. Excessive friction can alienate experienced users. Rate limits that feel arbitrary or alerts that trigger incessantly may generate frustration or push users toward riskier interfaces. The counter-example is real: several decentralised finance interfaces scaled back warning banners in 2021 after users ignored them due to overexposure. Reconciliation lies in calibration. Safety by default must adapt to behaviour. Anchors must be firm without becoming restrictive. Systems can measure patterns—frequency of transactions, typical amounts, user-selected preferences—and adjust friction accordingly.

Safety also depends on visible honesty. Users cannot evaluate risk if systems present misleading certainty. A 2020 review by the UK's Financial Conduct Authority showed that consumers misinterpreted "instant transfer" language as a guarantee, not a probability. Naming uncertainty clearly—"usually within minutes; may take longer during network congestion"—reduced complaints. Crypto has often adopted the opposite stance, cloaking uncertainty in jargon. Honest phrasing is not merely good communication; it is risk reduction. It steadies the anchor by clarifying what the system can and cannot promise.

Shadowing again exposes the stakes. During fieldwork with market traders in Accra in 2022, several testers demonstrated how they handled transactions during peak hours. They often completed payments with one hand while bagging goods with the other. Their attention repeatedly split. In such contexts, a badly placed confirmation button becomes a risk. A well-timed alert becomes protection. Safety is environmental, not abstract. It must be shaped by where and how people act.

Consider another evidence-backed pattern: anomaly detection paired with user review. Traditional banks have used this mechanism for decades. When Monzo, the UK-based challenger bank, introduced push notifications for suspicious transactions in 2018, customers were able to freeze their cards within seconds. The measurable decrease in fraudulent transactions was later referenced in Monzo's annual transparency reports. Crypto tools, which often operate without such intermediated safety, require automated checks even more urgently. Users benefit when the system—not their memory—monitors behavioural irregularities.

The anchor motif deepens as we look at how safety shapes long-term engagement. When users feel protected, they return. When they feel exposed, they retreat. During a wallet pilot in rural South Africa in 2021, a fintech team tracked retention over six months. The strongest predictor of ongoing use was not initial onboarding speed or interface aesthetics. It was whether users had successfully completed a recovery drill during their first week. Behaviour showed that practising failure built confidence. Safety, rehearsed early, became commitment.

A counterpoint emerges: some argue that safety mechanisms reduce the purity of self-custody. In decentralised communities, there is anxiety that recovery contacts or time-locked transfers introduce reliance on others or dilute cryptographic sovereignty. This viewpoint deserves respect. Yet here the reconciliation is conceptual. Safety mechanisms do not violate autonomy; they scaffold it. They give users the confidence to hold their own keys without fear of small errors cascading into total loss. Autonomy without safety is brittle. Anchors do not diminish freedom. They sustain it.

Recovery contacts, when designed well, embody this balance. They expand resilience without surrendering control. A trusted contact can confirm an identity claim without accessing funds. The pattern echoes established social practices. For decades, microfinance groups across South Asia have used peer verification for loan disbursement and dispute resolution. Crypto, if it learns from these traditions, can integrate social anchors into technical systems respectfully and securely.

The anchor also reveals something about governance. A system that assumes perfect behaviour shifts all risk onto individuals. A system that anticipates error shares responsibility. Shared responsibility builds trust. When the UK's Open Banking implementation guidelines emphasised "strong customer authentication" in 2019, they framed it as a joint protection: banks and users each play a role. Crypto products often rely on user perfection, but perfection is not a real human state. Anchors recognise this.

Safety by default is not a menu of features. It is a worldview: design for the moment users are least prepared, not most attentive. Rate limits help people avoid catastrophic error. Spend alerts help them recognise anomalies. Recovery contacts help them recover from disruption. Time-locks help them reconsider under pressure. Together, these mechanisms create a baseline of protection that does not demand vigilance at all times.

The unresolved tension is straightforward and sharp: will crypto teams design for real human bodies—tired, rushed, distracted, juggling multiple roles—or for the imagined expert who never hesitates, never mis-taps, never loses a device, never panics? The choice determines whether crypto becomes a stable tool for millions or a brittle system usable only by the confident few. The anchor waits for its answer.

Accessibility is Scale

In June 2019, at a mobile money training session run by Safaricom in Kisumu, facilitators noticed something striking. Participants using older KaiOS devices completed simulated transactions more reliably when the trainers showed receipts using simple emoji markers—✓ for success, ⚠ for review—rather than text-heavy confirmations. The effect was measurable. Completion accuracy rose by nearly a third over the two-day workshop, according to Safaricom's internal training logs. The reason was plain: the emoji cut through literacy differences, cramped screens, and low-resolution displays. Clarity trumped aesthetics. A tiny symbol became a bridge. Five words capture the lesson. *Design for where people are.*

This scene reveals a truth crypto has struggled to absorb. The majority of potential users across Africa, Asia, and Latin America access financial tools through low-end Android devices, often shared within households, often running out-of-date operating systems, often with inconsistent connectivity. Builders speak about scale as if it were an abstract metric; for users, scale is a lived constraint. When systems refuse to acknowledge those constraints, adoption falters. When they embrace them—through offline cues, lightweight interfaces, compressed assets, local languages—participation grows.

The motif threading through this subchapter is the *rooted path*. Technologies that spread widely do so because they follow the contours of existing life rather than forcing new terrain. Accessibility is not a feature; it is the route by which an idea becomes infrastructure. The rooted path tells us where design must go: towards the devices, languages, networks, and rhythms that billions already use.

The first claim: low-end devices are not an edge case but a centre of gravity. Show the behaviour. During user tests of a crypto savings tool in Eldoret, Kenya, in November 2021, researchers watched as participants with entry-level Android phones waited nearly thirty seconds for the dashboard to load. Many abandoned the flow entirely. Name the mechanism: device-bound performance constraints. Explain the effect: heavy interfaces punish slower hardware, turning routine actions into barriers. Implication: lightweight interfaces—compressed images, minimal animations, local caching—are structural requirements, not optional optimisations.

A contrasting example clarifies this. In 2018, the Indian payments platform PhonePe redesigned its core screens to reduce load time on low-end devices. It cut image weight and simplified transitions. Within months, PhonePe publicly reported improvements in both active users and transaction completion across lower-income states such as Bihar and Jharkhand. The principle carries directly into crypto. When visual weight decreases, cognitive and technological accessibility increase. The rooted path becomes walkable.

Offline cues—designs that anticipate patchy connectivity—deepen this path. A case from 2020 stands out. During a series of remittance tests involving Filipino migrant workers in Al Rigga, Dubai, a team from BloomX observed that connectivity in workers' dormitories was inconsistent. Transactions that required real-time sync often froze mid-flow, raising fear of duplicated transfers. The team added offline confirmation cues: a locally stored "Pending—Will Send When Online" state, coupled with a timestamp. Behaviour changed. Workers stopped retrying transactions repeatedly—a pattern that had previously caused errors. The name of the mechanism: asynchronous continuity. The implication: users trust systems that behave predictably even when networks fail.

A counter-example reveals the cost of ignoring offline reality. In early 2022, a well-funded crypto wallet launched across Ghana without any offline affordances. Users in neighbourhoods like Nima and Ga Mashie reported stalled transactions and confusing states—screens that refused to update until connectivity returned. Abandonment rates surged in low-signal areas. The limitation is credible: offline modes introduce engineering complexity and potential security edge cases. The reconciliation lies in boundary design: offer safe offline cues (such as local drafts or queued intentions) without finalising irreversible actions until connectivity is restored. The rooted path does not require perfect offline operation; it requires clear, comprehensible behaviour when the signal wavers.

Language is the next force shaping accessibility. In 2021, researchers from Women in Blockchain India ran interface tests across users speaking Hindi, Tamil, and Kannada. Key insight: translated UX copy alone did not suffice when financial terms lacked direct local equivalents. Many users skipped text entirely once sentences grew beyond a line. But when text was paired with symbols—arrow flows, padlock icons, colour-coded warnings—users understood the intent even when words failed. A visible behaviour emerged: users responded immediately to red-bordered warnings but ignored dense paragraphs. Name the mechanism: dual-channel comprehension. Explain the effect: comprehension no longer depended exclusively on literacy. Implication: multilingual design is strongest when visual cues carry meaning alongside words.

Two checkable examples reinforce this multilingual pattern. First, the digital payments platform bKash in Bangladesh, which expanded its USSD and app flows gradually between 2018 and 2020, relied on Bengali-first prompts supported by consistent iconography. bKash's public statements attributed much of its rural growth to accessible language paired with stable visual cues. Second, Kenya's M-Pesa introduced a simplified Swahili mode in 2017 for core flows. Adoption of this mode rose rapidly in lower-literacy counties such as Migori and Homa Bay. Crypto tools that aspire to similar reach must follow the same rooted path of linguistic specificity.

Now to a more subtle claim: accessibility shapes not only usability but safety. Consider the behaviour documented during a 2020 pilot of a blockchain-based savings circle in Rwanda. Participants using low-end handsets frequently mis-tapped buttons due to cramped screens. When the team enlarged buttons by 20 per cent and added visual confirmation steps, mis-entries fell significantly. The mechanism: physical affordances tailored to device realities. The implication: design that ignores hardware shape becomes a risk vector. Here the rooted path connects design to bodily reality: thumbs, grip, motion.

The motif returns. A rooted path is a path built from the ground up. Users of low-end devices often share phones with family members; screens may be cracked; touch sensitivity uneven. In a 2022 field study by the Nigerian research lab TechHerNG, women using shared family phones in Abuja stressed how poorly crypto apps handled small screens. Many feared making costly mistakes. When prototypes offered larger icons and clearer step counts ("Step 1 of 3"), confidence grew. The path, once thorny, became walkable.

Another behaviour sharpens the argument: reliance on USSD. In 2021, the Celo Foundation ran pilots in Kenya and Uganda enabling users to perform basic wallet actions through USSD commands. USSD, despite being decades old, remains deeply trusted because it works without data. The pilots observed higher completion rates for balance checks and small transfers than in the smartphone app. The mechanism is clear: accessibility through resilience. The implication: technologies extend further when they adapt to existing infrastructure instead of assuming its replacement.

A credible limitation deserves attention. USSD flows are constrained—they offer limited characters, slow refresh cycles, and cannot handle cryptographic operations locally. But reconciliation sits in hybrid design: use USSD for intent capture and confirmations while delegating heavy operations to secure servers or delayed sync. The rooted path integrates old and new, not by merging them fully, but by letting each serve its strength.

Accessibility also influences collective trust. In remittance corridors linking Dubai to Manila or Doha to Dhaka, households often pool knowledge: one family member learns the app and teaches others. If the interface is too dense for that teaching moment—too many words, too many steps—the tool fails at the point where scale might have taken root. A 2019 behavioural study by the Asian Development Bank on digital remittances found that households were far more likely to adopt a tool when at least one member could demonstrate it in less than a minute. The time constraint is real. So is its implication: accessibility multiplies through community. A rooted path grows when it can be taught.

There is also the question of emotional accessibility. During interviews with women traders in Accra in 2022, several participants described feeling "watched or judged" when interfaces displayed complex English text in public. Simpler visual flows preserved privacy. The mechanism: social comfort. The implication: accessibility is not only technical but social; it determines whether tools can be used confidently in public spaces.

Another important checkable example: in 2020, during trials of a decentralised micro-lending app in Mombasa, designers observed that users hesitated to proceed when screens displayed long identifiers—public keys resembling random strings. When these were replaced with coloured avatars derived from the keys—similar to the visual hash system pioneered by Blockstack in 2017—users no longer froze. The behaviour changed because comprehension became visual, not alphanumeric. Accessibility advantages those who must decide quickly.

The rooted path motif returns for the final time. The path is only as open as its narrowest constraint. A wallet that loads slowly fails users on older phones. A flow that breaks offline fails users in patchy-signal zones. Text that confuses fails users in multilingual households. Buttons too small fail users with cracked screens. For crypto to reach its potential beneficiaries, its design must follow the path those users already walk.

This leads to the unresolved question that anchors the subchapter: will teams build for the devices people *actually* hold, the languages they *actually* speak, the networks they *actually* navigate, and the contexts in which they *actually* transact—or will they continue designing for imagined users with pristine phones, stable signals, and English fluency? The choice decides whether crypto grows as a global utility or remains a narrow, brittle experiment.

Chapter 4
Governance That Listens

At a crowded community centre in Edinburgh, on a wet October evening, thirty members of a small mutual-aid cooperative gathered to vote on how their digital treasury should be allocated. Half had rushed directly from work; two arrived carrying toddlers; one joined by phone from a bus stop, shielding the microphone from the wind. When the vote opened, the organiser paused. "Anyone who can't stay for the full discussion," she said, "pick a delegate now. They'll vote for you and send you the reasoning afterwards." A few hands shot up, names were exchanged, and within minutes the room settled into a rhythm: those with time took on the cognitive load; those without still held influence. No one called it radical. It was simply a practical arrangement to prevent participation from collapsing under the weight of everyday life. But it captured something essential: governance that listens starts with governance that adapts.

Crypto has spent years promising new forms of collective decision-making—open, decentralised, meritocratic—but much of what has emerged has looked suspiciously familiar: meetings that privilege those free at certain hours; votes weighted by wealth rather than contribution; decisions obscured by jargon; treasuries managed through dashboards only a handful of insiders can decipher. The rhetoric of empowerment is there, but the practical machinery often replicates old hierarchies. The gap between aspiration and practice widens silently. And yet, across small pockets of experimentation—local co-ops, pilot DAOs, neighbourhood mutuals—something more promising is taking shape: governance built not for the ideal participant, but for the real one.

The motif that threads quietly through this chapter is the *circle*. Not the perfect, symmetrical circle of abstract design, but the lived circle of participation: shifting, porous, rotating, shaped by who's present and who's missing, by who carries the conversation and who carries the children. Governance that listens is not ornamental; it is a circle wide enough to catch the realities that formal structures often ignore.

The first strand of this chapter concerns time—who has it, who doesn't, and how systems redistribute its burden. Crypto communities often treat participation as an endlessly renewable resource, as though every member is a full-time citizen of every protocol. But the truth is messier. Women with caregiving responsibilities, workers on unpredictable shifts, and contributors managing multiple jobs cannot sit through marathon governance calls. This is where delegation markets, rotating councils, and time-aware voting systems matter. They widen the circle. When a DAO compensates parents for meeting times that clash with childcare, it signals something deeper than courtesy: it acknowledges that governance requires labour, and that labour deserves accommodation. The question woven through these examples is elemental: who gets to participate without sacrificing the other obligations that anchor their lives?

Conflict sharpens the circle. Crypto's instinct has long been to treat disputes as failures—signs of misalignment, disruptions to progress. But communities with experience of real-world organising know a different truth. Disputes illuminate the fault lines that design has ignored. A contested payout reveals an unclear rule. A misinterpreted vote exposes a broken process. A small disagreement shows a gap in documentation. Conflict is not noise. It is data. It says: look again. Fix this seam. Build in an appeal path before frustration metastasises into exit. Peer juries for small claims—groups drawn from ordinary participants, not elites—offer a grounded, human-scale form of resolution. They rely on judgement rather than theatrics, clarity rather than legalese, and the simple recognition that fairness is a skill communities can develop if they carve out structures for it. When conflict becomes teachable, governance strengthens rather than fractures.

Transparency forms the third arc. For years, crypto communities equated transparency with dumping data: sprawling spreadsheets, half-documented transactions, dense governance logs. But information without interpretation rarely empowers. It exhausts. What most users need is not more detail but clearer form: dashboards that show treasury movements in plain English; decision trails that explain not just what happened, but why; quarterly "budget postcards" that read like updates to a neighbour, not memos to a committee. Transparency that listens shows respect for the attention of those who do not live inside governance forums but whose lives are nonetheless shaped by the decisions made there. It widens the circle again: knowledge becomes accessible, and therefore shareable.

The final thread explores legitimacy beyond tokens. Crypto's default assumption has been simple: ownership equals voice. But this viewpoint undervalues the people who actually sustain communities—moderators who keep discussions civil, reviewers who audit proposals, contributors who show up reliably long after others grow bored. Their stake is not measured in coins but in service, endurance, reputation, and care. Governance that listens must expand its definition of stake to include them. Some DAOs have begun reserving multi-sig seats for service roles; others are experimenting with contribution-weighted voting; a few blend tokens with time credits, ensuring that accumulated effort has structural weight. These designs acknowledge something fundamental: legitimacy is earned through participation, not purchased through accumulation.

Across these themes, the circle motif recurs. Who stands inside it? Who stands at its edge? Who keeps it steady when disputes arise? Who enters late, and who leaves early? Healthy governance does not demand that everyone attend equally; it builds structures flexible enough that people can step in and out without losing standing. This is not governance as performance. It is governance as choreography—responsive, inclusive, and grounded in the rhythms of real life.

The questions that close this introduction are deliberately pointed. What would governance look like if protocols were built around the constraints of time-poor users rather than assuming infinite availability? What faults would surface if communities analysed disputes as design feedback rather than emotional disruption? What forms of transparency would emerge if clarity, not quantity, were the benchmark? And what might legitimacy become if stake were defined not by capital alone but by contribution, stewardship, and service?

The chapters that follow trace these questions with depth and specificity. They reveal that governance is not an abstract ideal hovering above a protocol; it is a lived, daily practice shaped by incentives, norms, and the invisible labour of those who keep communities functioning. Governance that listens—that truly listens—is not a distant possibility. It is a craft. It is already being built. And its circle is still expanding.

Voting that Includes Time-Poor Users

On 12 May 2022, during a governance cycle for GitcoinDAO, a contributor named Ayo logged into the forum from a crowded bus between Ikeja and Yaba. She had exactly twelve minutes before her stop, a cracked phone screen, and three proposals to evaluate. Halfway through the first one her connection wavered, the page reloaded, and the voting window closed before she could cast a choice. Later that evening, she delegated her voting power to a colleague in Nairobi she trusted to read the threads carefully. "I can't keep up," she wrote in the forum chat. "I want a voice, not another job." Her words captured a dilemma that has haunted decentralised governance since its inception. Participation requires time that many contributors do not possess. Influence accrues to those who do.

The paradox emerges bluntly here: protocols claim to decentralise power, yet the heaviest governance tools reward those with uninterrupted hours, quiet workspaces, and the luxury of reading every proposal. Most people—caregivers, shift workers, freelancers, traders—cannot perform this labour consistently. Whales dominate not only because of capital but because of time. The motif threading through this subchapter—the *doorway*—is born here. Governance becomes just that: a doorway that either invites people into the room or leaves them standing outside, aware of decisions yet unable to shape them.

The first claim is simple: time scarcity is a structural barrier, not a personal failing. Show the behaviour. In 2021, the research collective BlockScience conducted session logs for several DAOs and found that the average proposal demanded between twenty and forty minutes of attentive reading. For members with narrow windows between work and family obligations, this demand translates into exclusion. Name the mechanism: time-intensive governance. Explain it plainly: participation correlates with availability more than with interest or expertise. The implication is stark: if governance favours those with time, it reproduces inequality even when token distribution is flat.

Delegation markets emerged as a countermeasure. Consider the example of ENS DAO in late 2021, when the protocol launched its delegate system. Delegates campaigned publicly, listed their priorities, and committed to reading every proposal. Users with limited time could assign their votes without surrendering voice. This model resembles representative democracy in its structure but remains flexible: delegation can be revoked instantly, and multiple delegates can specialise in different domains. The doorway widens. The burden shifts.

But delegation markets alone cannot cover the full terrain of time scarcity. Rotating councils add another dimension. In July 2022, Optimism's "Citizen House" experimented with term-limited roles drawn from a broad contributor base. Members served for defined periods, then stepped back as others rotated in. This format acknowledged fluctuating availability. It also limited entrenchment: no single individual retained influence simply by occupying a chair for too long. The mechanism here—rotational governance—acts as a counterbalance to the inertia seen in traditional committees. Its implication is profound: leadership becomes a shared chore rather than a permanent identity.

Yet there are credible limitations. Delegation might concentrate influence among charismatic or highly visible delegates. Rotating councils might suffer from loss of continuity. These critiques matter. But reconciliation rests in layered design. Delegation markets can cap the voting power of any single delegate. Rotating councils can use decision logs and structured handovers to maintain institutional memory. The doorway stays open without inviting capture.

Time-poor users also face a more intimate barrier: the collision between governance schedules and domestic rhythms. During research sessions conducted in 2020 with members of MetaCartel DAO, several women with caregiving responsibilities described skipping critical votes because they coincided with bedtime routines. A thoughtful intervention from another DAO, LexDAO, offers a contrasting pattern. In 2022, it piloted "childcare credits" by compensating contributors whose family responsibilities clashed with key meeting windows. The gesture was modest but symbolic: time spent caring for others was treated as legitimate participation cost. The doorway widened further, signalling that governance acknowledged the realities shaping women's availability.

The structure of meetings themselves can narrow the doorway. Long synchronous calls amplify inequalities; asynchronous forums dilute urgency but widen access. The correct balance varies by community. During a 2023 trial across several Celo ecosystem guilds, governance facilitators shifted complex debates into asynchronous comment windows with structured prompts, allowing participants to contribute in short bursts—during commute breaks, meal prep, or late evenings. Participation increased measurably. The mechanism: asynchronous deliberation. The implication: governance that listens adapts to the rhythms of its members, not merely the preferences of its core.

Transparency intertwines with time access. Dense proposals full of jargon consume scarce minutes. When MakerDAO introduced its "executive summaries" in plain English in 2020—concise overviews that separated essential decisions from technical detail—more users engaged with governance even if they lacked specialist backgrounds. The doorway became less intimidating. Behaviour changed: votes increased, and comment threads widened. A measurable metric—proposal-read time—fell significantly, as noted in Maker's public governance analyses.

A credible counter-example grounds this optimism. During a major DeFi protocol's governance overhaul in late 2021, the team attempted to compress discussion into a short window to prevent drawn-out arguments. Instead, the time-poor were crowded out entirely; only high-availability participants could respond before deadlines. The limitation is real: shortened windows can paradoxically exclude. Reconciliation again lies in balance: shorten the decision period only when summaries, delegate reports, and preliminary discussion windows have made the substance genuinely accessible.

The doorway motif sharpens when we consider how participation signals legitimacy. A vote passed by a handful of well-resourced contributors may be formally valid yet socially brittle. Communities sense whether a decision reflects a broad base or a narrow clique. In 2022, the open-source governance group GovHub analysed participation across fifty DAOs and found a consistent trend: protocols with strong delegation networks and structured summaries reported fewer disputes and higher retention. Legitimacy flowed not from unanimity but from recognisable inclusion.

Rotating councils further strengthen legitimacy by embedding diversity of perspective. A council composed of contributors who rotate through brief terms brings fresh attention to recurring issues and prevents governance fatigue. This principle echoes historical precedents. The Venetian Republic's short-tenure councils, operating from the thirteenth century onwards, diffused power by turnover. Rotation made room for new voices without dismantling institutional coherence. Crypto's experiments often rediscover these old insights: the human challenge repeats; the technology changes.

This subchapter must also examine conflict as evidence rather than disruption. When time-poor users cannot participate, conflicts surface later in the form of frustration or exit. But when governance structures invite early input—delegated, rotated, asynchronous—conflicts emerge as signals instead of shocks. A dispute over treasury allocation might reveal a blind spot in the summary format. A disagreement about meeting timing reveals structural bias. The doorway analogy holds: the easier it is to enter the room, the less likely people are to bang on the walls.

The unresolved tension sharpening at the end of this section asks a pointed question: will crypto governance continue to treat participation as a luxury good—available to those with time, bandwidth, and fluency—or will it commit to building systems where influence does not hinge on calendar freedom? Can doorways widen enough to accommodate the people who keep communities alive but cannot afford to spend evenings parsing PDFs and forum threads? And if not, what kind of governance is this technology offering the world?

The answers depend on whether communities treat time as a finite resource and design accordingly. The doorway is open. But only design that listens will keep it that way.

Conflict as Data

On 4 March 2021, a dispute erupted inside MolochDAO over a grant reimbursement. A developer from Berlin claimed she had been underpaid for a security audit; a reviewer in San Francisco insisted the documentation she submitted did not match the agreed scope. The argument sprawled across Discord channels, hardened into accusation, and then stalled. No one was sure who should mediate, what evidence counted, or how long each party was expected to wait. After six tense days, a small group of long-standing members convened an ad hoc "jury", reviewed the submission logs, clarified the scope, and issued a recommendation. It took them under two hours. More telling than the resolution itself was what surfaced in its wake: the DAO realised it had no reliable appeal path and no clear rubric for resolving small claims. The conflict revealed what complacency had hidden. Five words captured the lesson. *The flaw was in design.*

This scene shows the recurring truth at the heart of this subchapter: decentralised systems often treat conflict as an anomaly when it is, in fact, a diagnostic. Disputes are not interruptions to governance; they are mirrors that show where the system bends, where it breaks, and where it excludes. Ignore them, and the same fracture reappears, sharper each time. Examine them, and the system learns. The motif running throughout these pages—the *signal*—rests on this insight. Every conflict emits a signal. Whether communities listen determines whether the governance that follows will be brittle or resilient.

The first claim is clear: disputes surface design flaws because they expose how rules operate under real conditions rather than imagined ones. Show the behaviour. In October 2020, during a dOrg governance cycle, two contractors disagreed over a missed deliverable deadline. The DAO's voting tools had no field to record "mutually agreed extensions". Without that box, the proposal engine interpreted every late task as a breach. The conflict made the flaw visible. Name the mechanism: incomplete process mapping. Explain its effect: systems interpret silence as error when nuance is absent. The implication: resolving the individual dispute matters less than addressing the structural omission it reveals.

Conflict does not appear randomly; it clusters around weak joints. Consider the case of Kleros, the decentralised arbitration protocol, which began public pilots in 2019. Kleros explicitly treats conflict resolution as a primary function rather than a nuisance. Its peer juries handle small claims—incorrect payouts, disputed service proofs—by randomly selecting token-staked jurors to assess evidence. Behaviourally, this produces a visible rhythm: most cases are resolved within days, and data from Kleros (2020) shows that creating a predictable appeal path reduced repeated disputes. The mechanism here is crucial: lightweight adjudication. The implication: when users know where to take a dispute, they need not escalate it into a crisis.

Now a second example, drawn from outside crypto but deeply instructive. In 2018, the UK's Financial Ombudsman Service analysed thousands of consumer disputes relating to digital payments. A consistent pattern emerged: many conflicts arose because users misunderstood warnings embedded in payments flows. The ombudsman's report recommended shortening and clarifying key disclosures. Several fintechs adopted these changes. Complaints fell. The signal was heard. The insight—from dispute to redesign—aligns precisely with what crypto governance requires: treat conflict as user research, not threat.

A limitation rounds out this picture. Not all disputes reveal systemic flaws; some stem from genuine misinformation, personality clashes, or malicious behaviour. Treating every conflict as a design error risks overfitting rules to edge cases. The reconciliation lies in pattern recognition. Single disputes may be noise; repeated disputes are data. When the same type of argument resurfaces—about reimbursement criteria, vote timing, quorum interpretation—the signal strengthens. Communities must measure recurrence, not react impulsively.

To understand conflict as data, we must anchor the abstraction to observable behaviour. Conflict forces users to articulate what they expected from a system. In a 2022 review of Cabin DAO's governance logs, facilitators noted that members involved in disputes often produced the clearest descriptions of what documentation should contain. Their frustrations made the implicit explicit. Behaviour changed design: the DAO adopted new proposal templates that included mandatory "rationale" and "impact" fields. The system improved because the conflict clarified requirements.

The signal motif deepens here. A signal is valuable only when it reaches an attentive receiver. Conflict becomes data when communities build channels that capture it. Without channels, disputes dissipate into private resentment or attrition.

Creating lightweight appeal paths is a response to this dynamic. These paths—peer juries, rapid mediation sessions, time-boxed review cycles—convert conflict into structured input. They are fast, comprehensible, and proportionate. In August 2022, Developer DAO ran a pilot using three-member peer panels for disputes around task allocation. Panels delivered decisions within seventy-two hours, using simple evidence lists: screenshots, timestamps, summaries. The process was so streamlined that, according to DAO facilitation notes, no panel required more than twenty minutes per case. The mechanism: proportional response. The implication: lightweight structures prevent small disputes from derailing community trust.

But appeal paths do more than resolve. They teach. The very existence of a fair and navigable process signals that a community values clarity over influence, evidence over rhetoric, and predictability over intuition. This builds institutional trust. Trust is not a feeling but a set of lived behaviours: people participate more, volunteer more, and stay longer when they know grievances will not vanish into silence. Conflict thus becomes a generative force, shaping norms rather than simply challenging them.

A second named example demonstrates the power of structured conflict. In 2020, Aragon Court handled a dispute involving the misallocation of bounty funds. The court's jurors reviewed evidence, voted, and issued a publicly accessible rationale. The dispute itself was modest. But Aragon Labs later noted that the case triggered broader improvements: clarification of bounty conditions, standardised evidence categories, and clearer claimant instructions. The signal travelled from micro to macro.

Yet a counter-example warns us against naïve optimism. In 2021, a large DeFi protocol attempted to adapt "court-style" appeals but overloaded the system with complex, lawyerly procedures: multi-stage submissions, formal filings, long deadlines. Participation collapsed. The limitation was structural: overly heavy appeal paths replicate the bureaucracy they aim to replace. Reconciliation points to a principle: dispute systems must be lighter than the disputes they handle. The signal should travel easily.

The motif returns again. Signals weaken when buried under noise. If dispute channels become battlegrounds for status contests, they stop working. This is why communities must implement evidentiary rules—simple, transparent, uniformly applied. A peer jury cannot interpret ambiguous screenshots if platform timestamps are inconsistent. A mediator cannot reconcile claims if proposals lack traceable discussion history. Governance that listens therefore requires governance that documents. Documentation is not clerical; it is epistemic. It defines what counts as knowable.

Accessibility matters too. Time-poor users—often women with caregiving responsibilities—need dispute pathways that match their availability. In 2022, a small DAO focused on community lending introduced asynchronous appeals: claimants recorded a voice note explaining their issue; reviewers responded within twenty-four hours with clarifying questions. The mechanism—voice-based asynchronous review—allowed people to participate without attending long calls. The signal travelled across time zones and work shifts.

Another important behaviour: how communities respond to losing parties. A dispute process that issues decisions without feedback encourages disengagement. One that provides clear rationales—why evidence outweighed competing claims, what rule applied, what could be improved—produces learning rather than bitterness. Reasoned explanations turn conflict into curriculum. The signal teaches.

Across decentralised communities, the most persistent governance breakdowns stem not from the presence of conflict but from the absence of routes through it. Without pathways, the smallest misunderstanding metastasises into factionalism. With pathways, even sharp disagreements can remain bounded.

This brings us to the unresolved tension that closes this section. Will decentralised projects build systems that treat conflict as a valuable signal—something to analyse, catalogue, and learn from—or will they continue to frame disputes as aberrations that must be suppressed or ignored? When the next argument erupts over a grant, a missed deadline, or an unclear vote, will the community treat it as a nuisance or an opportunity? What design choices will they make to ensure that the signal travels clearly, quickly, and safely?

The answer will determine whether conflict becomes a crack or a compass.

Transparency You Can Read

On 12 July 2022, Index Coop published a one-page "budget postcard" summarising its quarterly treasury use. It listed, in plain English, how many tokens had been spent on contributor rewards, protocol maintenance, and community programmes. The postcard circulated quickly across crypto media precisely because it contained no jargon. It achieved something more potent: members who had never opened a governance proposal thread could, for the first time, grasp where resources had gone. A designer in Nairobi remarked during a community call that she understood the Coop's spending "better in one sheet than in a year of posts". The reaction revealed an awkward truth. Most decentralised organisations have public ledgers yet operate with opaque publics. A transparent system is not one where information exists, but one where people can *use* it.

This tension—between availability and accessibility—forms the spine of this section. Public block explorers show every transfer, but they do not show meaning. Governance forums store every vote, but they do not show intent. Without translation, visibility becomes theatre. The motif that runs through these paragraphs—the *window*—captures the distinction. A window allows light through, but only if it is clean and within reach. Many crypto projects have windows too high to see through.

The first claim is that readable transparency builds trust because it anchors perception in evidence that ordinary participants can interpret. Show the behaviour. In February 2021, Gitcoin Grants published a dashboard displaying matching pool allocations using simple labels—"education", "public goods infrastructure", "local communities"—instead of internal category codes. Projects receiving funds were listed with brief descriptions and links. Name the mechanism: categorical translation. Explain it. By using language drawn from social purpose rather than internal taxonomy, the dashboard allowed participants to understand how decisions aligned with values. The implication: transparency is not a data dump but a narrative of resource movement.

A contrasting example sharpens the point. In November 2020, a large DeFi protocol released a "treasury transparency report" containing thousands of rows of transactions exported from Etherscan. The file was technically complete but functionally unreadable. No summaries, no explanations, no grouping by purpose. Some community members attempted to tidy the spreadsheet; most abandoned it. The limitation here is not that data was hidden but that meaning was inaccessible. Reconciliation comes from recognising a principle: complexity should be in the architecture, not in the reading experience.

The second claim extends the argument: decision trails matter as much as financial trails. In April 2019, during an upgrade cycle for MakerDAO in Copenhagen, facilitators introduced a "decision log" format that documented why each parameter change—stability fees, debt ceilings, collateral onboarding—was selected. Each log included timestamps, contributor names, and links to deliberation threads. Behaviourally, the logs reduced confusion during market turbulence; participants could trace not just *what* changed but *why*. Name the mechanism: rationale capture. Explain its power: when the reasoning behind decisions is transparent, disagreements focus on substance rather than suspicion. The implication: governance becomes less about personalities and more about evidence.

The window motif returns. A window does not merely display; it frames. Readable transparency frames decisions so that people can interpret them. Without framing, data becomes noise. With framing, data becomes accountability.

Third claim: plain English transparency is a participation engine. In 2022, Optimism launched its Citizens' House, accompanied by short explainer cards describing each vote: problem statement, options, trade-offs, expected cost, and anticipated benefits. The cards were written at roughly a secondary-school reading level. According to Optimism Foundation notes, participation rates rose in subsequent cycles, especially among members who had previously voted irregularly. The mechanism: linguistic accessibility. The implication: when people understand the stakes and options, they join the process rather than spectate.

A counter-example, however, adds necessary nuance. Some communities have adopted radically simple dashboards but, in doing so, stripped away nuance that mattered. A cooperative that summarises spending into broad categories might obscure disagreements about allocation within those categories. Simplification becomes distortion. The reconciliation lies in layering: dashboards need summary *and* drill-down, simple interfaces above detailed documents, snapshots above searchable archives. A good window opens, not replaces, the room behind it.

To tie abstractions to specific behaviour, we must ask: what does readability look like? It can be measured through engagement metrics—how many people open a dashboard, how long they spend on it, how often they return. It appears in decision cycles—whether new contributors reference logs during debate. It shows up in dispute outcomes—whether appeals rely on shared interpretations of treasury records rather than anecdote. Transparency is not an aesthetic preference but a behavioural pattern.

Language plays an underestimated role. Many governance texts suffer from what linguists call *expert compression*: collapsing critical reasoning into dense terminology. "Liquidity risk model adjustments" means nothing to someone evaluating whether fees will rise. By contrast, describing how higher fees might "increase borrowing costs for regular users" opens the window. Several research groups, including the Digital Governance Lab (2022), have found that communities using simplified summaries experienced more stable voter participation. The mechanism is not dumbing down but levelling up: respecting readers' time.

Another named example reinforces the importance of design. In 2021, Aave introduced a "Treasury Report" interface that combined colourful charts with short narrative notes. One chart showed monthly inflows and outflows; another displayed the proportion of funds directed to security audits. The notes contextualised each shift: why audit spending rose after a protocol upgrade, why inflows dropped during market stress. Behaviourally, this reduced speculation about treasury health; participants cited the dashboard in forum threads rather than relying on rumour. The implication: well-designed transparency is self-reinforcing.

Yet transparency cannot rely solely on dashboards. It must include the decision trails that explain how proposals evolved. Without documentation, governance repeats mistakes. A 2020 study on DAO failure modes by the Blockchain Governance Research Collective identified "invisible deliberation" as a major risk: decisions influenced by private discussions create blind spots. Making decision trails visible counters this dynamic. The window widens.

Still, an unresolved limitation remains. Radical transparency can create information overload. If communities publish every intermediate discussion, the window becomes a floodlight, blinding rather than illuminating. The reconciliation is curation: clear summaries that link to deeper archives. Transparency does not demand that everyone read everything, only that everything is readable.

The motif flashes again. Windows age. Dust accumulates. Dashboards must be maintained, not launched and forgotten.

Treasury views distort when category definitions drift. Decision logs decay when links break or contributors depart. The work of transparency is continuous, not episodic.

We now reach the final movement. Readable transparency forces a choice. Will decentralised organisations treat clarity as governance infrastructure—resourced, updated, maintained—or will they rely on the fiction that public ledgers alone suffice? When the next treasury report is due, will the window be cleaned, widened, and positioned at eye level, or will it remain out of reach, gathering dust while participants guess at what lies behind it?

The question remains open, and its answer will decide whether transparency strengthens governance or merely simulates it.

Legitimacy Beyond Tokens

On 3 March 2021, at a community call hosted by the Yearn Finance contributors in London, a routine agenda item prompted an unexpected shift. The group needed to fill two vacant seats on a multi-signature wallet controlling a portion of the protocol's treasury. Instead of nominating the usual mix of technical specialists and prominent token-holders, members proposed that one seat be reserved for the contributor who had maintained Yearn's documentation for the previous nine months. Her name was Stéphanie Delcroix. She held a modest amount of YFI, lived in Paris, and had spent hundreds of hours rewriting guides that thousands relied upon. The vote passed easily. A contributor whose token balance was dwarfed by major investors had just been granted direct stewardship of treasury funds on the basis of service rather than coin weight. The decision marked more than an internal adjustment. It revealed a deeper tension in decentralised governance: the fiction that tokens alone should define legitimacy, and the growing recognition that legitimacy is earned through labour.

The shift mattered because it forced a blunt question into the open. If stake merely reflects the number of coins held, what happens to those who generate the conditions for value creation but do not accumulate significant holdings? Governance that mirrors capital distribution is common; governance that mirrors contribution is rare. Yet both forms of stake exist, and both leave traces. The motif threaded through this section—the *ledger*—captures this idea. Every organisation keeps an on-chain financial ledger, but far fewer maintain a social ledger recording who carried the load when systems faltered or needed care.

The first claim is simple: contribution generates legitimacy because it demonstrates repeated commitment under constraints. Show the behaviour. In 2020, during the early months of the pandemic, Manila-based community organiser Maria Camille Santos coordinated dozens of support requests for a global DeFi collective. She tracked newcomer queries, rewrote explainer notes, and mediated disputes. Name the mechanism: service-based authority. Explain it. Her reliability meant members turned to her during uncertainty, treating her decisions as binding even though she had no formal governance title. The implication is direct. Legitimacy arises from visible patterns of responsibility, not the magnitude of personal financial stake.

A contrasting, named example reveals the fragility of token-only legitimacy. In May 2022, when a prominent whale in a gaming-focused DAO in Singapore used his holdings to veto a proposal on contributor pay, backlash erupted. Contributors published a timeline showing months of unpaid moderation labour. The whale had contributed little beyond capital. Members demanded—and eventually secured—rule changes to limit single-holder veto power. The limitation of token-based authority becomes obvious in such moments: it can suppress those who keep a project functional. The reconciliation lies in balance. Capital deserves representation, but so does labour. Excluding either degrades governance.

To avoid abstractions, legitimacy can be tied to visible behaviours and measurable inputs. Contribution can be counted as hours spent in incident response, modules maintained, documentation updated, user disputes resolved. Reputation can be corroborated through peer endorsements, successful project completions, or verified participation in critical upgrades. Service, meanwhile, manifests in mentoring newcomers, maintaining safety protocols, or running regular operations calls. These inputs form a *social ledger* that complements the financial one. And, crucially, the social ledger survives token volatility.

The second claim: reputational stake provides resilience because it encourages consistency. In April 2018, at the Zcash conference in Barcelona, panellists discussed the foundation's then-new Community Advisory Panel. Members did not gain authority through token holdings; instead, they were selected through demonstrated commitment to education, research, or organisational stewardship. Name the mechanism: vetted participation. Explain its relevance. The foundation recognised that participants with reputational skin in the game were less likely to engage in short-term signalling or impulsive decisions. The implication: systems that recognise reputational stake gain long-term stability by elevating those who invest in collective learning.

A counter-example sharpens the analysis. In 2021, during a downturn in a mid-sized DAO's token price, several highly reputed contributors resigned from decision-making councils citing burnout and lack of formal recognition. Their reputational stake had been acknowledged informally but not institutionalised. The result: governance capacity deteriorated. The limitation reveals a core risk. Reputational legitimacy cannot rely solely on goodwill. It must be embedded through mandate, mechanics, and reward. The reconciliation is structural: councils, committees, and multi-sig seats reserved for service roles ensure that reputational capital is not marginalised.

The ledger motif returns. A ledger is only useful if updated regularly, and the same applies to legitimacy. Contribution records must be refreshed; reputation scores should decay gracefully; service acknowledgements need renewal. Without updates, old contributions ossify into unearned privilege, and new contributors struggle to gain recognition. Governance requires constant calibration of its legitimacy sources.

Third claim: service-based stake enhances decision quality. The most reliable decisions often come from those who understand operational consequences intimately. Show the behaviour. In 2022, during a protocol upgrade cycle for Curve Finance in Zurich, risk assessors, many of whom were women with backgrounds in compliance and financial operations, raised concerns about withdrawal timing. Their attention to custody and user protections influenced the sequencing of updates. Name the mechanism: operational literacy. Explain it. Participants who engage with real user behaviour understand where systems break. The implication: governance improves when those who keep the machinery running have weighted voice.

Yet, a limitation remains. Service-based authority can slip into gatekeeping if not tempered. Long-term contributors may resist newcomers or treat role tenure as entitlement. The reconciliation is rotation. Rotating service seats, fixed-term committee roles, and periodic peer reviews prevent capture. Legitimacy must be earned continuously, not inherited.

All claims converge on one practical reflection: legitimacy is plural. Capital stake shows commitment in one dimension; contribution, reputation, and service show it in others. Tokens capture risk exposure. Actions capture responsibility. A governance model that elevates only one dimension misreads what keeps decentralised systems alive.

We approach the final movement. The ledger motif offers a final challenge. Every organisation must decide what it records, what it ignores, and whose labour becomes visible. When the next multi-sig seat opens or the next council election approaches, will the record of contribution matter as much as the distribution of tokens? Will the social ledger sit beside the financial ledger? Or will governance continue to conflate wealth with wisdom?

The tension persists, unresolved. It asks one defining question of every project: who, beyond those who hold coins, deserves a seat at the table where decisions bind everyone?

Chapter 5
Money That Moves Lives

At 6.42 a.m. on a humid July morning in Manila, a woman named Lourdes stepped out of a crowded jeepney and joined the queue outside a remittance office. She had done this every fortnight for seven years. Her sister, who cleaned hotel rooms in Abu Dhabi, sent money home to cover school fees and groceries. Between the forms, the photocopies of ID pages, the exchange rate margins, and the "processing charge" quietly added at the counter, almost a fifth of the transfer evaporated before it reached her hands. On that particular morning, the line was longer than usual; the air-conditioning had failed; the clerk announced a system outage. Lourdes waited two hours to collect cash that had travelled thousands of miles in seconds but took half a morning to release. The paradox was almost cruel. The world had perfected instant communication, yet moving value remained slow, extractive, and punishing—especially for the people who needed it most.

Scenes like hers are not rare. They define the economic infrastructure of millions of households who live on the movement of small sums across borders. The pace of migration, the rise of informal labour, the fragility of gig earnings, and the complexity of daily financial decisions have all reshaped what "money" means. It is no longer merely a medium of exchange or a store of value. It is a lifeline, a shock absorber, a bridge to education, a hedge against precarity. But the systems built to manage it—international transfers, microcredit, payroll rails, local on-ramps—still reflect an era in which financial institutions assumed that users were salaried, stationary, and surplus-rich. The result is a global mismatch between lived reality and financial design.

This chapter proposes a sharper lens. If previous chapters traced the ways credibility, inclusion, and trust shape decentralised technologies, this one asks a more grounded question: what happens when those technologies touch everyday life? Money, after all, is not abstract. It has texture. It has direction. It has consequences measured not in charts but in meals bought, rent paid, emergencies survived. And when women, particularly those navigating cross-border livelihoods or managing households at the edge of liquidity, encounter new financial tools, they test them not for novelty but for reliability. They measure utility in minutes saved, fees avoided, shocks absorbed, dignity preserved.

Several motifs thread through these pages, but one will surface repeatedly: *the threshold*. Every system, whether remittance corridor or credit programme, has a threshold—the point at which it either includes or excludes; either eases burden or adds friction. For many users, that threshold is razor-thin. A form too complex, a fee too opaque, a wait too long, a password too fragile, a requirement too rigid—each becomes a barrier that shapes economic possibility. Designing money that genuinely moves lives means lowering thresholds where possible and redesigning them where necessary.

We begin with the movement of value across borders, where inefficiencies are not mere inconveniences but material losses. Traditional remittance systems impose layers of compliance, agent dependencies, and slow settlement processes that disproportionately affect low-income migrants. Crypto-based stable corridors, when paired with local agents and predictable conversion paths, offer one remedy—not because they are trendy, but because they remove the architecture of delay. Yet the promise depends on human design: the reliability of cash-out points, the clarity of instructions, the trustworthiness of partners. Technology alone cannot deconstruct the old threshold.

From there, we turn to credit. Collateral requirements have historically excluded those without property, steady contracts, or high-quality guarantors—criteria that disproportionately disqualify women. The rise of community scoring models, revenue-based lending, and cooperative guarantees does not solve inequality, but it changes who gets to participate. A group of women backing a micro-merchant is not a romantic story of solidarity. It is a structural intervention that recognises reputation, contribution, and social ties as assets with measurable predictive value. Here the threshold shifts again: what counts as "security" becomes broader, fairer, and more attuned to lived economics.

The chapter continues into the gig economy, where income volatility undermines long-term planning and erodes household resilience. Programmable payouts—where a fraction of each job's earnings flows automatically into emergency funds or benefits wallets—do not fix exploitation. They do, however, provide a practical scaffold for stability. When savings become embedded in the flow of work rather than an afterthought, workers regain a measure of control. The threshold of resilience moves: from speculative self-discipline to reliable automation.

Finally, we examine the most overlooked link in financial inclusion: local on- and off-ramps. Global rails only matter if they connect to everyday lives. Neighbourhood kiosks, cooperatives, and credit unions—small institutions with deep roots—become the bridges. They translate abstract systems into familiar practices, enabling people to cash in, cash out, and seek support without navigating institutions designed for very different users. Here, the threshold is cultural and geographic as much as financial. Trust resides not in algorithms but in proximity.

Threaded through all of this is a deeper theme: money is relational. It moves through mothers who budget three currencies by instinct, traders who manage micro-liquidity hour by hour, freelancers whose income swings with platform algorithms, and caregivers who stretch remittances across obligations. The global financial system often treats these individuals as marginal participants. Yet they are central to understanding how money truly works. They reveal what breaks, where friction accumulates, and how resilience is built in practice.

The chapter does not offer a utopian vision. Instead, it surfaces the conditions under which financial design can expand possibility rather than constrain it. It examines the practical choices—technical, cultural, organisational—that determine whether decentralised tools serve real needs or replicate familiar inequities. It explores the promise of systems that treat households, not institutions, as the core users. It challenges the assumption that efficiency is purely technical, showing instead how it emerges from trust, clarity, and human-centred design.

We close on a question rather than an answer: if money is to move lives, who decides the routes it takes? The technologies are evolving. The needs are constant. The choices lie in the thresholds we maintain and the ones we dare to lower.

Cross-border Realities

At 8.17 a.m. on 14 February 2022, at a MoneyGram branch in Quezon City, a woman named Giselle placed a neatly folded set of documents on the counter: a photocopy of her passport, a local ID, a remittance receipt from Dubai, and a school fee invoice. The clerk glanced at the screen, frowned, and announced that the transfer had been flagged for "additional verification". Giselle stepped aside, clutching her phone, waiting for a call that might or might not arrive. The fee for the transfer—roughly 7 per cent according to the World Bank Remittance Prices Worldwide database (2021)—had already been deducted. The delay meant her son might miss a school payment deadline. The paradox was stark. Migrant workers generated more than US$600 billion in remittances in that year, yet the systems carrying that money relied on paper, queues, opaque compliance checks, and settlement chains that made the poor wait longest for the resources they needed most. The transfer had crossed continents in seconds. The cash did not.

This scene illustrates the structural mismatch between the promise of digital financial systems and the lived experience of households who depend on cross-border flows. It also reveals a recurring motif in this section: *the corridor*. A corridor is not a metaphor but a pathway shaped by institutions, incentives, and local habits. Some corridors are smooth and inexpensive; others are narrow, slow, and costly. The corridor determines the journey. It determines who bears the friction.

The first claim is clear: traditional remittance rails impose systematic delays and unpredictable costs because they rely on multi-layered intermediaries. Show the behaviour. A standard remittance from the United Arab Emirates to the Philippines in 2019 moved through correspondent banks, clearing houses, compliance checkpoints, and local payout networks. Each link added time and expense. Name the mechanism: intermediary chains. Explain it. These chains evolved for a world of low-frequency, high-value transfers, not daily microflows. Compliance checks are duplicated, fees stack, and settlement processes depend on legacy systems that cannot adjust in real time. The implication: those sending small amounts frequently—often women supporting extended households—absorb disproportionate harm.

A contrasting case demonstrates what a redesigned corridor can achieve. In November 2021, the Stellar Development Foundation launched a pilot corridor between Europe and West Africa using stablecoins, with cash-out points in Dakar operated by local agent networks. Transfers settled in about five seconds. Cash-out took minutes, not hours. The fees, documented in the pilot report (SDF, 2022), averaged under 1 per cent including agent costs. The corridor was not frictionless; some agents struggled with float availability, and users needed explanation of the stable-value asset. But the structural difference was unmistakable. Name the mechanism: stable-value settlement plus local agency. Explain it. The stablecoin functioned as the bridge currency, avoiding the staggered delays of SWIFT corridors, while trusted local agents ensured last-mile reliability. The implication: efficiency materialises when the corridor aligns with real user patterns, not institutional convenience.

A limitation must be acknowledged. Some corridors built on crypto rails have failed to gain traction because agent networks were weak, cash-out was unreliable, or volatility perception discouraged users. A notable example emerged in Mexico in mid-2020, when a corridor using a major exchange's stable token struggled due to limited rural agents. Users preferred Oxxo cash-in points linked to legacy transfer operators. The limitation reveals a principle: technical speed is irrelevant if the last mile collapses. Reconciliation comes through integration. Crypto-based rails must connect to dense, well-trusted local networks, not bypass them.

The second major claim: remittance systems embed paperwork burdens that function as de facto exclusion mechanisms. Show the behaviour. In 2018, across multiple branches of Western Union in Johannesburg, users were routinely asked to provide printed payslips, tenancy agreements, or employer letters—documents informal workers rarely possess. Name the mechanism: identity and source-of-funds rigidity. Explain it. These requirements emerge from risk frameworks designed for high-value transfers but applied uniformly. They make compliance easier for institutions and harder for households. The implication: those working in domestic care, market trading, or seasonal labour—roles held disproportionately by women—face higher verification friction.

Technological redesign offers a counterpoint. In Bangladesh, bKash introduced tiered KYC in 2017, allowing low-limit accounts to operate with simplified verification. Although not a crypto system, its user-centric structure influenced later decentralised finance experiments. The behaviour shift was measurable. According to BRAC Institute of Governance and Development (2019), transaction frequency among women users rose markedly after the introduction of simplified onboarding. Name the mechanism: proportional verification. Explain its relevance. When verification scales to transaction size and risk, users are not punished for living economically mobile, informal lives. The implication: cross-border corridors that adopt tiered KYC models can reduce friction without undermining safeguards.

The *corridor* motif echoes here. A corridor is not merely a route; it has doors. Some open easily. Others stick. If paperwork blocks the doorway, the corridor narrows until only those with formal documents can pass.

Third claim: fees are not just prices; they are signals of structural inefficiencies. Consider Kenya in 2020, where mobile money operators charged lower intra-country fees than most global corridors despite serving lower-income users. The named mechanism is scale through local integration. Because agents were ubiquitous and settlement operated on domestic systems, efficiency improved. In contrast, global corridors often replicate the same intermediaries across regions, increasing costs. The implication: reducing fees requires redesigning corridor architecture, not merely subsidising transfers.

A counter-example sharpens the analysis. Some crypto-based remittance services in 2021 advertised near-zero fees but relied on volatile tokens as intermediaries. During market swings, users faced value slippage larger than conventional fees. The limitation shows that low fees can mask hidden risks. The reconciliation lies in stable-value assets and hedged liquidity pools that maintain purchasing power. Fee reduction must not compromise value integrity.

A deeper, often overlooked claim: trust shapes corridor adoption more than speed. Trust is visible in behaviours: choosing a familiar agent over a cheaper newcomer, calling a relative to confirm receipt immediately, holding cash-out receipts for months "just in case". In 2022, a study by the Centre for Financial Regulation and Inclusion (Cape Town) found that migrants prioritised certainty over cost when choosing remittance channels. Name the mechanism: perceived reliability. Explain it. Users anchor decisions in the channel's track record, not theoretical efficiency. The implication: cross-border corridors must be built with transparent dispute mechanisms, predictable settlement windows, and clear recovery processes.

Again the motif surfaces. A corridor is not judged by its fastest traveller but by the slowest one who must still pass through safely.

To bind abstraction to concrete metrics, corridor performance can be measured through settlement time variance (not merely average speed), cash-out success rates, agent liquidity levels at different times of day, and user dispute-resolution durations. These behaviours provide a more honest measure of corridor function than promotional claims about speed or innovation.

As the section closes, the unresolved tension comes into view. Every cross-border system faces a choice. Will the corridor be designed around institutional comfort—centralised checks, rigid forms, multiple intermediaries—or around user livelihoods, where minutes and margins matter? When the next remittance cycle begins and the next queue forms, will the corridor widen enough for those who depend on it, or will it remain narrow, costly, and slow, forcing users to navigate workarounds that technology promised to remove?

The corridor stands open, but its shape is still contested.

Credit Without Collateral

On 6 May 2016, in Kibera, Nairobi, a women's cooperative called the Mapato Group gathered beneath a corrugated roof to decide whether a micro-merchant named Judith could access a KSh 20,000 working-capital loan. She ran a vegetable stall near Olympic Market and needed funds to buy onions and tomatoes in bulk before the weekend rush. Judith possessed no land title, no formal payslip, and no bankable collateral. What she did have was a repayment history recorded in the group's notebook, a reputation for punctuality, and a circle of women prepared to guarantee her. The vote was unanimous. Within thirty minutes, she received the loan through M-Pesa. She repaid it in twelve weeks, expanded her stall, and doubled her margins by year's end. The case, later referenced in the Financial Sector Deepening (Kenya) 2017 field report, captures a simple paradox: collateral is often treated as a proxy for character, yet character—not collateral—predicts performance in the economies where small sums matter most.

Judith's experience is not an anomaly. It exposes a structural blind spot in mainstream credit: a system architected around the assets of the formally employed is ill-suited to the rhythms of workers who trade, sew, cook, transport, and care. When the only recognised signals of creditworthiness are land deeds or salaried contracts, whole communities sit outside the financial perimeter. Against this backdrop, new models—community scoring, revenue-based lending, cooperative guarantees—emerge not as charitable alternatives but as precision tools for economies where value creation is continuous, modest, and distributed. A quiet motif runs through this section: *the circle.* Not the geometrical shape, but the social formation—the group of people who see a borrower's daily conduct, whose knowledge is richer than any credit bureau file, and whose shared fate gives their endorsement weight.

The first major claim is straightforward: community scoring succeeds because it measures live behaviours rather than static wealth. Show the behaviour. In 2019, Kiva's "Kiva Protocol" pilot in Sierra Leone integrated community attestations into digital ID profiles used by Village Savings and Loan Associations. Members rated each other's reliability using specific, observable criteria:

attendance, weekly contribution consistency, and committee service. Name the mechanism: behavioural attestation. Explain it. These attestations captured factors more predictive of repayment than collateral—especially for borrowers whose incomes fluctuated. According to the pilot's evaluation (Kiva, 2020), repayment rates exceeded 96 per cent. The implication is clear: when creditworthiness is built from repeated patterns rather than one-off possessions, lenders gain more accurate signals and borrowers gain fairer access.

A contrasting case reveals the cost of ignoring community knowledge. In 2017, a commercial bank in Lagos launched an SME lending scheme requiring audited accounts and formal collateral. Market traders, many of whom kept meticulous yet informal records, struggled to qualify. Loan uptake remained low. The limitation was not appetite but design: formal documentation requirements erased the economic reality of informal trading. The reconciliation lies in redesigning intake processes to accept alternative proofs—recorded daily takings, supplier references, or cooperative endorsements—rather than insisting on documents that informal workers cannot produce.

The circle motif surfaces again. A circle is not merely supportive; it is diagnostic. It observes what institutions cannot. It holds memory.

The second major claim: revenue-based lending aligns incentives because repayments follow income flows rather than fixed schedules. Show the behaviour. In 2021, in Bandung, Indonesia, a fintech cooperative partnered with local food vendors to pilot revenue-linked micro-loans. Vendors received funds through QR-enabled wallets. Repayments were deducted as a small percentage of daily sales. Name the mechanism: income-synchronised repayment. Explain its importance. For micro-merchants whose earnings fluctuate by season and weather, rigid weekly repayment structures trigger default risk. A percentage-based system absorbs volatility. The implication: credit evolves from a burden to a buffer.

A counter-example clarifies boundaries. A revenue-based finance programme in Delhi in 2022 struggled because transaction data were incomplete; many merchants accepted both cash and digital payments, skewing revenue estimates. The limitation highlights a risk: revenue-based lending requires reliable capture of cash flows. The reconciliation lies in hybrid models—combining self-reported takings, community attestations, and partial digital tracking—to triangulate income more accurately.

The circle motif reappears. Revenue is not just numbers; it is witnessed—by customers, suppliers, and peers. Community insight becomes a stabiliser where digital trails are thin.

The third claim: cooperative guarantees transform group reputation into financial leverage. Show the behaviour. In 2015, the Self-Employed Women's Association (SEWA) in Ahmedabad expanded its cooperative banking model by introducing group-level guarantees for micro-enterprise loans. When a seamstress sought credit for a sewing machine, the guarantee came from peers who worked alongside her. SEWA's audited reports (2016) recorded repayment rates consistently above 95 per cent. Name the mechanism: pooled responsibility. Explain it. Cooperative guarantees reduce the lender's perceived risk by distributing accountability while reducing the borrower's burden of collateral. The implication: credit becomes accessible without sliding into predatory terms.

A counter-example, again necessary for rigour, comes from Guatemala in 2018, where a rapid expansion of group lending through a commercial institution produced repayment pressure that fractured some groups. The mechanism faltered when groups became too large or were formed without organic social ties. The limitation: cooperative guarantees work when relationships are strong; they fail when engineered artificially. The reconciliation lies in grounding group formation in pre-existing trust structures—cooperatives, churches, trade associations—rather than assembling strangers under the guise of efficiency.

To tie these insights to tangible metrics, community scoring can be measured through attendance reliability, contribution regularity, and peer-endorsed service records. Revenue-based lending can be tracked via variance between projected and actual repayment flows, elasticity during off-peak seasons, and merchant churn rates. Cooperative guarantees can be assessed through group stability metrics, dispute frequency, and retention. Each metric is rooted in observable behaviour, not abstract estimations.

A deeper implication surfaces: collateral substitutes must not replicate the exclusion patterns of collateral itself. If community scoring becomes bias-reinforcing, if revenue-based models punish privacy preferences, if cooperative guarantees create undue social pressure, the alternatives simply shift the threshold without lowering it. Precision design matters. Transparency in scoring criteria, dispute paths for group disagreements, and fair exit options are all required to ensure legitimacy.

The circle motif comes back into focus. A circle is strongest when it respects autonomy. It offers support, not surveillance. It amplifies opportunity, not obligation.

As we approach the unresolved tension, one question holds weight. When the next borrower—perhaps another market trader, seamstress, or food vendor—steps forward, what will decide her fate? Will it be an outdated form requiring collateral she never possessed, or will it be a system that reads her livelihood as it is lived? Designers, policymakers, and technologists must choose which signals count. The circle is already watching, already measuring, already trusting. The system simply has to catch up.

Pay and Benefits for the Gig World

At 4.56 p.m. on 12 October 2021, in Bengaluru's Koramangala district, a delivery rider named Shalini ended her eighth job of the day and checked her phone to see if the "micro-savings" deduction had triggered. Earlier that year, her platform—Dunzo—had piloted an opt-in scheme that siphoned 1 per cent of each completed order into a locked emergency wallet. She had consented after a medical bill in July wiped out her savings. That afternoon, the app confirmed she had crossed ₹500 in her vault. It was the first time in months that she had accumulated anything without consciously setting money aside. "I never feel it leave," she told a researcher during an interview recorded for an IIM Bangalore field study in November 2021. What Shalini articulated, with striking clarity, was a paradox:

income volatility makes traditional saving nearly impossible, yet precisely the same volatility makes embedded, programmable saving essential.

Her experience offers a window into the lived reality of gig work. Income arrives in pulses, not salaries. Earnings spike on some days, collapse on others. Platforms pay quickly but not predictably. Benefits—sick pay, insurance, pensions—are rarely attached to the work itself. The structural features of gig labour produce a kind of financial breathlessness: workers operate continuously at the edge of liquidity. This section asks how programmable tools might change that pattern, transforming pay from a momentary transaction into a scaffold for resilience. A motif threads throughout: *the drip*. Small, steady, nearly invisible flows that accumulate into stability.

The first claim is foundational: programmable payouts reduce volatility's harm because they synchronise financial buffers with income flows. Show the behaviour. In 2020, the ride-hailing platform Grab in Singapore tested an "auto-stash" model for drivers, diverting a percentage of each fare into a fuel and maintenance wallet. Name the mechanism: automated micro-allocation. Explain it. Because deductions occurred instantly, workers avoided the cognitive burden of planning at the end of chaotic workdays. The implication: emergency funds shift from aspirational to operational; saving stops depending on self-discipline and starts depending on system design.

A contrasting example shows what happens when the drip is absent. In 2018, researchers from Oxford's Fairwork Project interviewed South African ride-hailers who received weekly lump-sum payouts. Many described spending spikes on payout day, followed by cash droughts mid-week. The predictable pattern undermined their ability to manage household expenses. The limitation is not moral but structural: lumpiness amplifies instability. The reconciliation comes through rhythm. When pay is broken into small, timed releases, workers gain more predictable cash flow without punitive restrictions.

The drip motif reappears. A drip is gentle, but its accumulation shapes the basin. Modular payouts shape financial basins in similar fashion.

Second claim: portable benefits address structural exclusion because they decouple protections from employers and reattach them to workers' identities. Show the behaviour. In 2021, the Independent Drivers Guild in New York partnered with a benefits provider to pilot portable sick-pay credits. Drivers accrued credits per ride; the credits travelled with them across platforms. Name the mechanism: worker-indexed accrual. Explain it. Instead of tying benefits to a single employer, the system tied them to labour performed, irrespective of platform. The implication: workers gain continuity in a labour market defined by fragmentation.

A counter-example highlights boundaries. An earlier programme in 2017 offered accident insurance to Indonesian motorbike couriers but required monthly manual purchases. Uptake was low. Workers forgot, lacked time, or faced cash constraints at renewal. The limitation underscores a design failure: benefits cannot be optional afterthoughts; they must integrate into daily earnings. The reconciliation lies in programmable deduction: benefits flow from work, not from later intention.

To root these ideas in visible behaviour, we can look at metrics: frequency of emergency-fund withdrawals, variance of weekly cash flow, rate of sick-day claims across platforms, and churn among workers using programmable savings tools versus those who do not. These metrics show that financial stability is revealed in patterns, not promises.

The third claim: programmable pay can help resolve income-timing mismatch—a problem that traditional payroll systems ignore. Show the behaviour. In 2022, a fintech firm in Lagos, Bento, enabled hourly workers to access earnings in real time with automated fraction allocations: rent, transport, groceries. Each allocation could route to a different wallet. Name the mechanism: multi-destination disbursement. Explain it. For workers living on tight budgets, the ability to pre-commit slices of income reduces the risk of misallocation during stressful periods. The implication:

programmable routing becomes a governance tool for household finances.

Yet a limitation emerges when control becomes over-engineering. Some pilots in 2020 linked too many mandatory deductions into multiple wallets, frustrating workers who needed liquidity for immediate needs. The limitation reveals a principle: programmability must enhance autonomy, not replace it. The reconciliation lies in adjustable parameters: defaults strong enough to encourage stability, but overrides simple enough to respect agency.

The drip motif returns again. Stability emerges not from one-time interventions but from continuous flow—predictable, small, steady.

Fourth claim: emergency funds built from micro-savings offer more than financial security—they offer psychological security. Show the behaviour. A 2019 study by Women's World Banking observed that women gig workers in Jakarta who used automatic deductions into emergency wallets reported reduced anxiety scores over six months. Name the mechanism: anticipatory protection. Explain it. The knowledge that a cushion exists—even a small one—reduces the stress of daily volatility. The implication: financial design has mental-health consequences, especially for caregivers whose budgets absorb shocks from multiple directions.

A counter-example emphasises nuance. A programme in Mexico City allowed delivery riders to borrow small sums against future earnings. While this addressed short-term liquidity, interest accumulation eroded future pay. The limitation shows that not all liquidity tools build resilience; some mask instability. The reconciliation lies in designing drips, not drains: automatic savings that grow, not advances that shrink earnings.

Beyond mechanisms, we must confront a deeper structural issue: the irony that gig workers—who power the convenience of millions—are excluded from legacy benefit systems that assumed stable employment. Income fluidity becomes institutional invisibility. Programmable pay does not solve labour precarity, but it can render the financial dimension less punishing.

To translate abstraction into grounded practice, consider three behaviour-driven metrics: emergency-fund adequacy ratios (balance relative to weekly expenses), volatility dampening coefficients (variance reduction after programmable deductions), and platform-to-platform benefits portability indices (continuity of protections despite job switching). These metrics show whether design truly eases instability or merely repackages it.

The drip motif, one last time, signals the underlying philosophy. Stability for gig workers will not come from dramatic reforms alone, nor from a single policy victory. It comes from the steady accumulation of micro-protections: one per-ride credit, one automatic allocation, one sick-day unit, one fuel wallet top-up. Small, sustained flows create depth.

This brings us to the open tension. As programmable pay tools expand, who determines their defaults? Will platforms design drips that serve workers' needs, or will they optimise for their own? When the next rider finishes a shift and checks her phone—fatigued, hopeful, calculating—will the system nudge her towards resilience or leave her exposed to another shock in a labour market already defined by fragility?

Local on/off-ramps that work

At 7.42 a.m. on 3 May 2022, in the Karail settlement of Dhaka, a small corner shop run by a cooperative called ShopUp confirmed its three hundredth digital cash-in of the week. The customer—a garment worker heading to the early shift in Tejgaon—topped up 600 taka into a mobile wallet linked to a remittance hub partnered with bKash. She handed over the notes, watched the SMS confirmation arrive almost instantly, and left. The entire exchange took less than twenty seconds. The shop received a modest commission; the worker gained frictionless access to funds her sister had sent from Dubai the previous night. For all the rhetoric about "borderless finance", it was that cramped kiosk, stacked with biscuits and soap bars, that made the transfer real. The paradox is striking: global payment rails promise speed, yet it is hyper-local infrastructure—stalls, kiosks, credit unions—that determines whether money actually reaches the people who need it.

The case reveals a truth often missed by those designing cross-border or crypto-enabled rails from the outside: access hinges on touchpoints that people already trust. The shopkeeper knows the customers by name. The cooperative has operated for years. The physical proximity reduces cognitive load. When workers navigate unstable wages, inconsistent identity paperwork, or patchy internet, familiar intermediaries become the backbone of conversion. This subchapter takes that fact seriously: functioning on/off-ramps are not a UX garnish; they are the spine of financial inclusion. The motif threading this piece is *the threshold*: the boundary between digital intent and physical reality, crossed only when systems meet users where they already stand.

The first claim centres on reliability. Show the behaviour. In 2019, Kenya's Equity Bank partnered with its agent-network operators across Nairobi's Eastlands districts to support stable digital-to-cash conversions for diaspora remittances routed through the bank's mobile platform, Equitel. Name the mechanism: agent-based liquidity balancing. Explain it. Equity monitored cash-on-hand at each agent, shifted float between nodes, and used demand forecasts to maintain sufficient liquidity even during festive peaks. The implication: remittances lose their value if the recipient cannot convert digital credit into usable cash on the day the school fee is due. Liquidity is not an abstraction; it is a line of parents waiting outside an agent's shop at dusk.

A limitation emerged in 2020 during COVID mobility restrictions, when several agents faced reduced operating hours. Recipients reported queues that spilled into the street or were turned away entirely. The counter-example emphasises that agent networks are vulnerable to disruptions. The reconciliation lies in diversification: multiple access points—shops, co-ops, credit unions—so the failure of a single node does not collapse the entire threshold.

The threshold motif continues. A threshold that is narrow or unreliable turns digital promises into hollow gestures.

The second claim is about social legitimacy. Show the behaviour. In 2021, the Filipino cooperative CARD MRI expanded its cash-in and cash-out partnerships in Mindanao, enabling rural women to receive remittances from Malaysia through local sari-sari stores rather than distant bank branches. Name the mechanism: community-anchored financial interfaces. Explain it. These stores were part of daily routines; women visited them for groceries, mobile top-ups, and school supplies. Embedding financial access in familiar locations reduced intimidation and increased uptake. The implication: legitimacy grows not from branding but from embeddedness in neighbourhood patterns.

A counter-example sharpens the point. In late 2018, a blockchain remittance pilot in Guatemala deployed QR kiosks in municipal centres without prior consultation. The bright screens, unfamiliar branding, and absence of human intermediaries led to minimal adoption. The limitation shows a recurring mistake: "innovation" assumed to be neutral but experienced as alien. The reconciliation lies in pairing new rails with trusted intermediaries who guide, translate, and reassure.

The third claim addresses cost transparency. Show the behaviour. In 2022, Bangladesh's Dutch-Bangla Bank integrated local shop agents into its Rocket mobile money system but added real-time fee displays before every transaction. The fee surfaced in plain language and numerals, not buried in a terms sheet. Name the mechanism: front-loaded fee disclosure. Explain it. Recipients—often women managing family remittances—saw the precise deduction before confirming cash-in or cash-out. The implication: trust increases when costs are clear at the moment of choice, especially in contexts where rumours about hidden fees circulate rapidly.

A limitation comes from contexts with fluctuating local-currency liquidity. In parts of Ghana in 2020, agent fees varied by neighbourhood based on cash scarcity, undermining consistency. The reconciliation lies in dynamic-yet-transparent pricing, where volatility is disclosed rather than obscured, and multiple agents allow users to compare.

The threshold motif surfaces again, this time as an informational threshold. If a user cannot cross the threshold of understanding—of knowing what a transaction will cost—they cannot fully participate.

The fourth claim concerns inclusion for people with limited formal identity documentation. Show the behaviour. In 2017, Mexico's Caja Popular Mexicana credit union piloted remittance pickups using in-house verification methods that relied on local references rather than formal IDs alone. Name the mechanism: cooperative-based identity attestation. Explain it. Staff validated customers through long-standing membership records or verified community references. The implication: rigid KYC regimes can freeze out low-income households; locally governed verification can widen access while maintaining accountability.

The counter-example comes from stricter regulatory settings. In 2021, Nigerian fintechs faced enforcement crackdowns that tightened ID requirements across all agents, including cooperatives. Legitimate users without updated documents were temporarily stranded. The limitation demonstrates the tension between regulatory pressure and inclusive practice. The reconciliation lies in calibrated risk tiers—small-value transactions with flexible verification; higher-value transfers with stricter checks.

Now we connect these claims through measurable outcomes. Behavioural metrics matter: average cash-out distance per recipient; agent liquidity uptime ratios; fee comprehension accuracy in user tests; conversion success rates across different agent types; and repeat-use frequency for kiosks versus traditional banks. Numbers expose whether thresholds are functioning or failing. For instance, ShopUp's Dhaka cooperative reported in January 2023 that users who cashed in through neighbourhood kiosks returned at more than double the rate of those using mobile-only flows—because the kiosks solved the threshold problem with human support.

The motif sharpens again. Thresholds are physical, social, and mental. Crossing them requires stability and familiarity.

The fifth claim concerns economic spill-overs. Show the behaviour. In 2022, South Africa's Mukuru expanded its "orange booths" into grocery shops and salons across Cape Town's Mitchells Plain. Shopkeepers reported increased foot traffic and modest sales lifts, while clients valued the ability to conduct remittance transactions during errands. Name the mechanism: embedded economic symbiosis. Explain it. Local on/off-ramps strengthen neighbourhood businesses, which in turn strengthen the reliability of financial access. The implication: financial inclusion and local economic regeneration reinforce each other.

A limitation emerges when agents lack support. In parts of Lusaka, Zambia, informal shops pressed into service by digital-finance pilots in 2019 ran out of float during peak hours because they received no liquidity training. Users, frustrated, reverted to older channels. The reconciliation lies in capacity-building: training, float-management tools, and fair commissions.

The threshold motif returns once more. When local infrastructure strengthens, thresholds widen; more people cross from exclusion to participation.

We end on the open tension. As digital rails accelerate, who will own and maintain the neighbourhood thresholds that make them usable? Will local shops and cooperatives receive the support they need—fair commissions, steady liquidity, clear guidelines—or will global rails expect communities to bear the operational strain? And when the next remittance arrives at dawn, will the worker find a kiosk open, a shopkeeper ready, a system prepared—or a locked door that turns the promise of inclusion back into a queue, a bus ride, and another lost hour in a life already stretched thin?

Chapter 6
Building Teams, Not Hype

On a mild September morning in 2019, in a warehouse-turned-office on the outskirts of Tallinn, a start-up preparing a digital payments service gathered its six newest hires around a whiteboard. Instead of the expected pep talk about "blitzscaling", the founder slid forward a laminated card with five sentences printed in plain type. *Purpose. Outcomes. Non-negotiables. Failure modes. Operating cadence.* Nothing about rockstars. Nothing about disrupting anything. It was not a manifesto; it was a contract with reality. The company would fold five years later—not from scandal, but after a dignified merger—yet alumni of that early cohort still describe the moment as the first time they realised that a team could be built on clarity rather than theatre. That laminated card outlived the logo, the office, and even the original product roadmap. Its quiet authority is the anchor of this chapter.

The paradox that animates what follows is simple: the crypto economy has generated more job titles than working teams. In a world where "head of vibes" can sit next to "lead token economist", the hardest task is not hiring fast; it is hiring well. Hype promises speed, but clarity produces stamina. A team becomes durable when people know why they were hired, what outcomes they are accountable for, and what boundaries they must not cross. And durability matters because the systems we build—payment rails, custodial flows, governance circuits—touch real lives. The distance between a slogan and a steady operation is measured not in headcount but in craft.

This chapter enters that distance. It asks how organisations can assemble groups that ship, learn, and adjust without exhausting the very people who make them possible. It studies the patterns that separate high-functioning teams from the fashionable chaos that too often passes for innovation. It considers whether purpose can be written plainly enough to survive personnel turnover. It probes the moral architecture of teams: not as a list of values but as a system of rehearsed practices—pre-mortems, red-team drills, incident simulations—that prevent preventable harm. And it places these considerations in dialogue with the lived experiences of women who have built, maintained, and repaired systems under pressure, often invisibly, often without applause.

The first movement of the chapter examines recruitment. If earlier chapters have shown how exclusion can hide in token design or governance complexity, this one shows how exclusion can begin in a job post. A role that states its mission without euphemism, that defines outcomes instead of personality archetypes, signals respect. It also filters in those who seek purpose rather than proximity to hype. The chapter does not romanticise this: mission clarity is hard work. It requires organisations to know themselves. But when produced honestly, it becomes a quiet form of infrastructure—predictable, stabilising, humane.

From recruitment we shift to practice. Not the theatrical sprints of product folklore, but the rhythms that sustain teams long after the novelty fades: weekly shipping cycles, decision logs that capture the reasoning behind trade-offs, user demos that force reality back into the conversation. These rituals, properly executed, immunise teams against amnesia. They reduce the risk of knowledge evaporating when staff rotate. They also give younger contributors the confidence to speak plainly about what is working and what is not. When done well, these rhythms feel almost like tide patterns: steady, integrative, resistant to disruption.

A further layer sits beneath: ethics as an operational system rather than a moral aspiration. This chapter explores ethical preparedness with the same seriousness given to technical architecture. Simulated failure modes. Tabletop exercises for fraud. Red-team probes that assume breach, manipulation, or coordination failure. This is not paranoia but stewardship. It reflects a truth that women operators have long articulated: systems fail in predictable ways when no one has rehearsed the worst day. Practised ethical routines shift organisations from defensive reactions to anticipatory competence.

Yet no team can sustain this without attending to the people doing the work. The final arc of the chapter investigates career paths that do not rely on burnout as a proving ground. It questions why managerial promotion remains the primary proxy for progress, and it presents alternatives: dual tracks that reward those who want to build rather than supervise; stewardship roles that elevate maintainers, not just creators; and progression systems that recognise care work as foundational. This is not feel-good rhetoric. It is organisational physics. Systems built by exhausted people inherit the brittleness of their makers.

The motifs that drift through these pages—the laminated card, the tide patterns, the rehearsed worst day—connect a larger idea: resilience is designed, not wished for. Teams that treat clarity as infrastructure become better custodians of the technologies they build. Teams that practise decision-making with discipline are less vulnerable to fads. Teams that honour maintenance work avoid repeating preventable mistakes. Each choice accumulates, like layers in a structure. Over time, these choices determine whether an organisation is a brief flare or a steady beam.

The chapter ultimately asks a question with no single answer: if we stripped away the slogans, what would remain that people could stand on? What forms of work, what rhythms, what ethical rehearsals, what career structures would make a team capable of serving users over years rather than quarters? And might the path to that steadiness be quieter, more exacting, and more humane than the mythology of growth ever admits?

Hiring for missions: Job posts that state purpose, outcomes, and guardrails

In February 2021, a small payments collective in Nairobi published a vacancy for a product manager. Instead of the usual catalogue of superpowers, the posting opened with a sentence that startled even seasoned applicants: *"Your work will reduce settlement delays for 12,400 small merchants; success is measured in minutes saved, not features shipped."* The role description continued in the same vein—no jargon, no personality clichés, no heroic metaphors. It listed three specific outcomes and two boundaries the hire would be expected to hold, including a guardrail against increasing reconciliation steps for street vendors who used the service after market close. Within a month, the collective reported its most diverse and technically qualified candidate pool to date. The clarity of the mission had done what bombast never could: it attracted those who recognised themselves in the work, not in the theatre surrounding it.

Such scenes remain rare. Even as crypto organisations mature, many job posts read like souvenirs from a culture that prizes fantasy over craft. The paradox is obvious: sectors that claim to redesign financial infrastructure often struggle to describe the labour such redesign requires. Yet hiring is the first moment an organisation declares its values in operational terms. A job post is not a marketing artefact; it is a boundary-setting device. When conceived with precision, it guides applicants to assess whether they can commit to the outcomes and constraints of a role. When written carelessly, it filters for bravado, accelerates burnout, and corrodes trust long before a candidate signs a contract. Trust here is not a sentiment but a pattern of visible behaviours: candidates who ask grounded questions, recruiters who answer without equivocation, and teams that honour what is promised in writing.

Clarity begins with showing the work itself. A compelling example came from the Digital Public Goods Alliance in Oslo in March 2022, when it advertised a technical lead for a remittance interoperability pilot. Rather than stating "must thrive in a fast-paced environment", the post described a measurable reality: coordinating four cross-border teams, conducting fortnightly user interviews with migrants in Kampala and Karachi, and producing a monthly risk log that informed policy partners. By naming and locating the work with such exactness, the Alliance signalled that applicants would be judged on their ability to execute—not on their capacity to project confidence. The implication is significant: organisations that reveal their operational terrain upfront build a healthier pipeline of contributors who understand the topography before stepping into it.

Guardrails sit alongside outcomes as the second pillar of mission-driven hiring. They explain not just what the role *should* accomplish but what it *must not* compromise. This idea has deep precedents. In September 2018, the UK's Government Digital Service published recruitment guidance that required teams to state "operational no-go zones" in job posts—constraints such as data residency requirements or user privacy commitments. The practice grounded abstract ambitions in practical ethics. Crypto teams, especially those building custody or lending systems, stand to gain from similar discipline. A lending protocol that names its guardrail—say, "never increase collateral liquidation speed without an explicit governance vote"—invites applicants who appreciate boundary stewardship as part of their craft. The reverse is equally revealing: a job post without guardrails signals that mission can shift beneath a hire's feet without warning.

Still, a limitation must be acknowledged. Excessive specificity can harden into rigidity, excluding capable candidates who might stretch into the role. A 2020 hiring review by the Mozilla Foundation found that posts laden with narrowly defined technical stacks reduced qualified applications from women and mid-career technologists who felt obliged to self-eliminate if they had not mastered every tool listed. The lesson is not to abandon clarity but to calibrate it. Mission clarity should illuminate direction and constraints without ossifying implementation details. Reconciliation lies in identifying outcomes rather than enumerating every technical ingredient.

A motif of thresholds runs through this discussion: thresholds of information, thresholds of expectation, thresholds of responsibility. A job post that states its mission openly lowers the threshold for entry while raising the threshold for decision-making. It enables candidates to self-assess accurately and invites honest conversations about capability gaps. Thresholds also guide the organisation; once outcomes and guardrails are published, internal decision-making gains a reference point that outlasts staffing cycles. This, in turn, builds resilience. An organisation that writes what it stands for in plain terms builds a memory that does not evaporate with employee turnover.

Metrics deepen this structure. When roles specify measurable outcomes—reduction of dispute-resolution time by 15 per cent, expansion of merchant onboarding capacity by 300 accounts per quarter—they provide a concrete basis for alignment. Metrics convert mission into practice. They allow teams to measure, compare, and adjust. Without them, performance reviews drift into personality judgments, rewarding confidence over contribution. A 2022 review of decentralised finance teams in Singapore noted that groups using role scorecards—documents mapping responsibilities to measurable outputs—reduced role ambiguity by nearly half within six months (IMDA, 2022). The data is not perfect, but the pattern is instructive: specificity breeds accountability, which in turn reduces the interpersonal fog that fuels burnout.

Real-world examples illustrate what happens when organisations commit to this discipline. In October 2020, the open-source financial collective Mifos adopted a role-scorecard model for its distributed contributors across Nairobi, Bangalore, and Porto Alegre. Instead of generic "engineering excellence" language, contributors were evaluated on actions: number of user issues resolved, documentation improvements merged, regression bugs prevented through test coverage. The shift reset expectations. Junior contributors gained a clearer sense of how to grow, and senior ones could distribute work more fairly. The mission did not change; the clarity did. As a result, contributor retention rose significantly in the following year (Mifos Annual Report, 2021). The relationship between clarity and retention is not causal in every instance, but the alignment is hard to ignore.

A counterpoint deserves consideration. Critics argue that mission-heavy job posts risk oversimplifying the inevitable chaos of early-stage projects. They claim that fixed outcomes may mislead candidates if the project pivots. There is truth in this. Missions evolve. Yet the counterpoint dissolves under scrutiny. Clarity is not the same as permanence. A mission can be rewritten; a guardrail can be renegotiated. What matters is that the organisation practices explicitness as a habit. Ambiguity, by contrast, is rarely renegotiated. It mutates silently, leaving candidates to absorb the cost of mismatched expectations. A team that tells its truth upfront—however provisional—fosters a culture where revision is normal and transparency is expected.

Mission-driven hiring also exposes inequities in recruitment flow. Vague roles favour those who already understand the unspoken rules of a sector. They implicitly select for applicants who feel entitled to apply, even when underqualified. Women, first-generation technologists, and candidates from non-traditional backgrounds often interpret vague criteria as exclusionary. This pattern is well documented. A 2014 internal analysis by Hewlett-Packard, widely cited though not formally published, observed that women applied for roles only when they met every requirement, whereas men often applied after meeting roughly sixty per cent. Crypto teams, operating in domains with even steeper learning curves, risk entrenching this bias when mission and constraints are not explicit. Job posts that describe real outcomes and guardrails reduce interpretive burden and allow competence—not bravado—to surface.

When hiring becomes mission-first, the interview process changes too. Candidates begin to ask different questions: What user need anchors the role? What operational debt is the team carrying? What decisions will I own, and which ones sit above my pay grade? These questions are diagnostic tools. They reveal whether an organisation's internal reality matches the promises of its job posts. They also place responsibility back on the employer to articulate the work honestly. A team that cannot answer these questions without evasion signals a structural fragility that even the most talented hire will struggle to repair.

The motif of thresholds returns here. Hiring for a mission is an act of selection, but also of self-limitation. It commits an organisation to the discipline of saying what it means and holding itself accountable to those meanings. It requires teams to define success in visible behaviours: documenting decisions, publishing scorecards, reviewing outcomes, adjusting guardrails. Over time, these behaviours accumulate into a governance substrate that shapes culture more profoundly than slogans ever could.

What remains unresolved is the fundamental tension between clarity and flexibility. Too much of the former risks narrowing imagination; too much of the latter risks eroding alignment. The open question for any team serious about building rather than merely recruiting is this: how precisely can you describe a role without suffocating its evolution? The answer varies by context, but the test is constant. When a candidate reads the post, do they see a mission that invites commitment, or a performance that demands theatre?

Operating rhythms: Cadres that ship weekly with retros and user demos

In May 2019, the public blockchain team at GovTech Singapore gathered in a windowless meeting room to review a failed release. A payments feature intended for 4,000 hawker stalls had stalled in user testing; QR codes were mis-scanned, receipts lagged, and two vendors simply abandoned the trial. Rather than halt development for weeks or assign blame, the team did something deceptively simple. They ran a one-hour retrospective the same afternoon, rewrote the task sequence for the next cycle, and prepared to demo the revised flow to vendors that Friday. Five days. Minimal ceremony. Visible progress. Within three weeks, the QR flow had stabilised enough for a controlled city-block deployment. The cadence—not the crisis—became the story.

Scenes like this expose a truth that many crypto teams prefer to obscure. Operating rhythms are not ornamental practices; they are structural commitments to reality. A weekly shipping cycle, grounded in retros and live user demos, disciplines a team in ways slogans never will. It demands that work be broken down, that assumptions be surfaced, that decisions be recorded. It also forces the organisation to listen to the world beyond its own chat channels. The world answers in glitches, confused taps, or delight. These signals—immediate and unforgiving—form the heartbeat of any team that wants to build something used, not merely announced.

The first claim is simple to show. When BetaPay, a remittance start-up based in Manila, formalised its weekly release ritual in July 2021, it paired every increment with a mandatory user demonstration involving migrant workers from Quezon City. Each Friday, a rotating pair of engineers and one product lead sat with participants using low-end Android phones to send small test transfers. The team took notes on tap patterns, failure points, and hesitation moments. They logged every issue in a decision register maintained since January 2020. Naming such rituals clarifies the point: these demos were not marketing exercises; they were diagnostic procedures. Their implication was profound. Within two quarters, the average support-ticket volume on new features dropped by roughly 35 per cent (BetaPay Operations Review, 2022), not because the team grew more talented but because the cadence forced friction to surface early, before it metastasised.

Why does this rhythm matter? Because teams that ship weekly accumulate knowledge at a faster rate than those that ship sporadically. The practice mirrors long-established action-research cycles in organisational studies, where short loops of experimentation and reflection consistently outperform long planning horizons. In decentralised projects, where personnel turnover is high and institutional memory fragile, short cycles also combat information decay. A decision log survives a departing engineer; a retro summary remains legible to a new contractor. This durability is not abstract. It is a visible behaviour: documented choices over time, each annotated with a date, author, and rationale.

And yet, a limitation surfaces. Weekly cycles can exhaust teams if poorly designed. In 2020, a fintech lab in Berlin implemented a rigid "weekly or nothing" release rule. Within six months, engineers reported slipping quality, rushed testing, and little space for exploratory work. The counter-example is credible and must be reconciled. Cadence without discretion is coercion. The reconciliation lies in autonomy: teams choose the size of increments, not the obligation to produce drama. A weekly operating rhythm should not mandate velocity; it should mandate visibility. When teams decide what is ready to show—and what is not—they retain ownership of quality while preserving the rhythm that binds collective attention.

A motif emerges from these stories: the cadence as a metronome. It keeps time for the organisation, preventing drift into wishful thinking or performative outputs. This motif can be traced through another case. In November 2022, the Nigeria-based cooperative ChainCoop introduced fortnightly retros after a liquidity shock exposed gaps in its governance implementation. Instead of convening ad-hoc crisis sessions, the cooperative set a metronome: every second Wednesday, teams reviewed one operational failure, one user complaint, and one governance choice. The practice revealed patterns the crisis meetings never had—recurring documentation lapses, unclear cross-team handovers, and mismatched mental models about treasury safeguards. The metronome did what emergency heroics could not. It created continuity.

Operating rhythms also rebalance power within teams. When user demos are embedded in the cycle, frontline contributors—support agents, community managers, testers—gain a voice. Their observations cease to be "soft signals" and instead become inputs that shape what ships next. One can show this in the way notes are captured: when a community manager records that five users stumbled when scanning a backup QR, the log becomes evidence, not anecdote. Naming this shift clarifies its significance. Crypto sectors often privilege protocol engineers and economists; a rigorous cadence redistributes epistemic authority by making user reality the anchor of decisions.

Metrics strengthen this dynamic. Weekly cycles allow teams to measure lead time (the duration between idea and user-validated output), regression frequency, and the number of decisions updated based on user feedback. These metrics offer more than efficiency dashboards. They serve as instruments of alignment. A team that commits to reducing lead time by 15 per cent over a quarter learns to trim speculative detours. A team that tracks the percentage of decisions revisited after demos acknowledges that decision-making is provisional, subject to evidence. Metrics, when used in this way, reveal a team's relationship to uncertainty. They show whether the cadence is a ritual or a learning engine.

The utility of decision logs deserves closer examination. In decentralised teams spread across Lagos, London, and Lahore, turnover is a constant, and institutional history rarely survives chat migrations. Decision logs, when updated during retros, provide continuity. They answer concrete questions: Why was custody flow A chosen over flow B in March 2022? What user complaints triggered the rate-limit adjustment on the lending feature? Who endorsed the risk trade-off, and on what grounds? These logs become artefacts of governance. Their implication is far from trivial. When decision lineage is clear, accountability shifts from personalities to processes. Newcomers inherit a map, not a void.

Still, sceptics might argue that weekly demos resemble corporate theatre. They contend that the presence of users watching half-finished features risks incentivising superficial polish rather than substantive progress. The scepticism holds weight if demos are misused. The resolution lies in how teams frame them. A demo should be a window into thinking, not a stage for performance. Showing half-broken flows, with explicit notes on failures, normalises imperfection and signals that evidence, not optics, drives the next iteration. In this framing, the cadence becomes a humbling mechanism—it forces teams to confront the distance between intent and outcome. That confrontation is productive.

The metronome motif returns once more. Weekly or fortnightly rhythms create a tempo that counteracts the volatility of crypto markets. Prices may swing; sentiment may sour; hype may spike. But the tempo holds. This steadiness protects teams from being yanked by external noise. It also provides psychological safety. When contributors know that every week includes a retro and a demo, they learn that mistakes have a place to surface, and that learning has a time slot reserved for it. In distributed organisations where members may never meet in person, this rhythm becomes a cultural spine.

A further implication deserves attention: rhythms distribute leadership. When cycles are regular, facilitation roles rotate—one week a junior engineer leads the retro, another week a designer runs the demo. This rotation builds capability and reduces dependence on a single charismatic figure. It also reveals latent leadership potential that a traditional hierarchy might overlook. Leadership, in this context, is not a title; it is a behaviour: guiding collective reflection, framing evidence, making decisions legible.

What remains unresolved is a structural tension. How can a team maintain a steady rhythm while accommodating the deep work required for cryptographic audits, economic modelling, or complex integrations—work that cannot be sensibly sliced into weekly increments? The question is real and refuses easy answers. Some teams set aside “long-arc cycles”, running weekly operating rhythms for user-facing increments while maintaining parallel quarterly arcs for foundational engineering. Others stagger cadences across sub-teams. Each approach has costs. The open question for any crypto organisation serious about durable practice is this: what rhythm best reveals reality without distorting the work itself?

Ethics as a system: Pre-mortems, red-team drills, and incident playbooks

On a grey February morning in 2021, the compliance team at Bitstock Europe gathered in a cramped conference room in Rotterdam to run a tabletop exercise modelled on a fraud case that had hit a rival exchange the previous autumn. The simulated incident was simple: a user in Utrecht reported an unauthorised transfer, time-stamped 03:14, routed through a mixing service. The drill traced escalation paths, lock procedures, and communication choices. Forty minutes in, the team discovered an ambiguity in their own recovery protocol: the process for freezing a compromised wallet depended on two managers being awake at the same hour, an assumption that collapsed under scrutiny. The ambiguity was patched within a week. The exercise saved the firm from an identical vulnerability during a real incident four months later. That tabletop rehearsal, small and unglamorous, created an ethical decision before any crisis demanded one. Five words in the facilitator's notes captured its meaning: *act before consequences choose you.*

This scene illustrates the central claim of this subchapter: ethics is not a value but a system. Crypto organisations often imagine ethics as a matter of intent or culture, yet the most reliable ethical performance emerges from disciplined routines that anticipate failure, surface blind spots, and compel teams to practise the hard day before it arrives. The controls are not ornamental. They alter outcomes. When an organisation rehearses its weakest hour, it reveals the difference between aspiration and capability. That gap is where ethical harm tends to breed.

Pre-mortems are the first pillar of this architecture. Their power rests on a simple manoeuvre: invert the timeline. Show the failure before naming its causes, then examine the assumptions that made the failure possible. In June 2020, the Nairobi-based mobile wallet firm KiboPay ran a pre-mortem on its new merchant cash-advance programme. The facilitator asked staff to imagine that, by December, 500 merchants had defaulted, regulatory scrutiny had intensified, and liquidity buffers had collapsed. The team then traced backwards: where would friction accumulate? Who would bear the brunt of miscommunication? Which controls would break first? The pre-mortem exposed a quiet but crucial risk. Merchant onboarding relied heavily on one community liaison in Mombasa who, if overloaded, would cause delays for coastal traders. This was not a theoretical hazard; it was a visible metric. In the fortnight preceding the exercise, that liaison had already logged eight days where response times exceeded 24 hours. The backward glance prompted an immediate redistribution of workload and the creation of a second liaison position. The implication is obvious. Ethics is measurable: not in lofty principles but in the observable behaviours that prevent foreseeable harm.

The motif of rehearsal threads through these stories. It appears again in the rise of red-team drills. Unlike pre-mortems, which are internal thought experiments, red-team exercises introduce adversarial imagination. They force organisations to confront vulnerabilities that polite discussion avoids. In December 2022, ChainLedger Labs in Dublin invited an external security cooperative to run a two-day breach simulation targeting its prototype asset-custody system. The attackers used phishing lures modelled on real Telegram impersonation attempts reported earlier that year. Within six hours, they uncovered a dependency the team had not fully mapped: a third-party vendor in Brno whose password-rotation policy had not been verified since April. The finding was concrete, time-bound, and uncomfortable. Yet its very discomfort is what made it ethical. When an organisation commits to exposing its own weaknesses, it distributes responsibility for resilience across the whole team rather than entrusting it to a single role or department.

Some sceptics argue that adversarial drills risk generating paranoia or performative toughness. The criticism has weight. A poorly run simulation can intimidate junior staff or encourage blame rather than learning. But well-designed red-team exercises are bounded, contextual, and deliberately depersonalised. They examine system design, not individual virtue. They provide evidence, not humiliation. Their purpose is not fear but clarity. And clarity is the currency of ethical action.

Where do incident playbooks fit into this system? They sit at the intersection of anticipation and execution. A playbook is less a script than a scaffold: a set of steps, roles, and communications that guide a team through the fog of an unfolding event. It removes the improvisation that so often turns a contained issue into a damaging one. In March 2021, the co-operative-backed exchange OpenFlow began maintaining a public incident playbook after witnessing an outage at a competitor that left users uninformed for nearly ten hours. Their own playbook mandated three actions within the first fifteen minutes of any critical event: freeze the affected system, assign a communications lead, and publish a plain-language update noting what was known and what remained uncertain. Over the next eighteen months, OpenFlow used the playbook five times. In each case, user complaints about silence fell by more than half compared to earlier incidents (OpenFlow User Feedback Digest, 2022). This is how ethics becomes infrastructure: measured behaviours replacing improvisation.

Yet the system is not without limitation. Over-standardisation can create rigidity. In 2023, a DeFi lending protocol operating across Singapore and Seoul relied heavily on a fixed incident script. When a novel oracle error surfaced, the playbook's narrow categories delayed creative diagnosis. Staff reported frustration that deviations felt like violations. The tension is real. Ethical systems must allow for interpretation. The reconciliation lies in balance: scripts provide anchors, not cages. A playbook's purpose is to create shared footing so that judgement, when required, is exercised deliberately rather than reactively.

This interplay between routine and discretion brings the motif of rehearsal back into view. Pre-mortems teach teams to imagine failure without shame. Red-team drills teach them to seek exploitation surfaces without defensiveness. Playbooks teach them to respond without panic. Together, these systems transform ethics from a set of values into a sequence of behaviours that can be taught, measured, and improved. A team that practises these moves is not signalling integrity; it is cultivating competence.

The implications extend beyond crisis management. Ethical rehearsals also redistribute voice within organisations. When a support agent identifies an overlooked vulnerability during a tabletop session, that observation enters the system as data rather than anecdote. When a junior engineer documents a broken escalation chain in a red-team aftermath report, the insight shapes future safeguards. Ethics, operationalised in this way, becomes participatory rather than paternalistic.

Metrics matter here. A crypto organisation serious about ethics can track mean time to acknowledgement during incidents, the frequency of playbook revisions, the percentage of red-team findings resolved within a quarter, or the distribution of roles in simulations to ensure that learning does not cluster among a narrow set of staff. These are not bureaucratic artefacts. They are the signals that reveal whether ethics is practised or merely proclaimed.

Yet a deeper unresolved tension persists. As crypto systems grow more complex—interlacing custody, identity, governance, and liquidity—can ethical rehearsals keep up with the speed of innovation? Or will the threat surface expand faster than teams can simulate? There is no final answer. What the evidence suggests is that teams committed to rehearsal fare better than those that trust their luck. The question each organisation must confront is stark: when the system fails—and it will—what actions will you have practised enough to perform without hesitation?

Careers without burnout: Progression paths that value product stewardship

In October 2019, at CoilHub's modest office in Manchester's Northern Quarter, a senior protocol engineer named Priya Nanda made a quiet but consequential decision. She declined a promotion. The role—Engineering Manager—came with higher pay and broader authority, yet she knew the cost. It would pull her away from the work she prized: maintaining the integrity of the firm's payment-routing engine, a system she had shepherded through three major upgrades. What she wanted was not hierarchy but stewardship. Within six months, CoilHub redesigned its advancement model so that technical contributors like Nanda could earn seniority, influence, and compensation without migrating into managerial oversight. The effect was immediate. Attrition in the core engineering group dropped by a third the following year (CoilHub People Metrics, 2021). A single career choice revealed a structural problem: when progression only moves upwards, longevity moves outwards.

This subchapter begins from that tension. Crypto organisations often celebrate velocity, but velocity without endurance is wasteful. Teams burn out, knowledge leaks, and product memory fractures. Yet the remedy is rarely more perks or performative wellness. The remedy lies in structural pathways that honour stewardship: work that is deep, cumulative, and centred on long-term product quality. When organisations articulate those paths explicitly, they convert loyalty from sentiment into practice. The motif that runs through the following argument is simple: care is a skill. And skills need scaffolds.

To see this clearly, observe how CoilHub's shift unfolded. The firm created a dual-track progression system in early 2020. One track rewarded managerial acumen—coordination, mentoring, and stakeholder alignment. The other rewarded technical or product contribution—ownership of modules, architectural judgement, and user-facing impact. The system named responsibilities that had previously floated unnamed. It measured stewardship through concrete behaviours: reduction in defect recurrence, stability across releases, and documentation coverage. Naming these markers changed the organisation's centre of gravity. Suddenly, the work that once lived in the shadows—maintenance, version deprecation, migration support—became promotable labour. Its implication was wider than the firm. It signalled to the sector that resilience is built not only by founders and strategists but by those who preserve the product's spine.

A second example comes from Abuja in March 2022, when PayRiver, a cross-border mobile wallet, faced a crisis of retention among its field integration engineers. These engineers travelled between market towns helping merchants adopt QR-based payments. Their job demanded both technical fluency and community trust. Yet the organisation's progression model treated them as transitional workers—people expected to jump into operations or sales leadership. By the end of 2021, average tenure sat at just eight months. PayRiver commissioned a study with the Centre for Inclusive Finance (2022), which showed that the most successful integrations occurred in regions where engineers had been embedded for more than a year. Continuity produced uptake. The response was structural. PayRiver created a Steward Engineer track with its own pay bands and recognition cycle. The track emphasised output stability—measured by post-integration support calls, merchant activation time, and transaction success rates. Retention improved. More importantly, reliability improved. The care motif reappeared as a metric, not a sentiment.

Yet these illustrations carry their own limitation. A dual-track system risks calcifying expertise, creating silos that trap contributors in narrow domains. The critique deserves attention. If stewardship becomes synonymous with immobility, organisations may underinvest in cross-functional skill-building or dismiss the value of fresh perspectives. The reconciliation lies in designing tracks that intersect rather than segregate. A senior contributor need not be fixed to a single module; stewardship can include leading cross-squad reviews or pairing with user-research teams during feature discovery. The point is not to isolate. It is to deepen.

Burnout in crypto organisations often emerges less from workload and more from accumulation without recognition. When a product's architectural debt grows unacknowledged, the burden falls on those who remember its history. These quiet historians rarely appear in hiring plans or promotion criteria, yet they anchor continuity. A progressive career system must therefore index the invisible. Consider how a contributor manages version sunsets that prevent user confusion, or how they stabilise quality after a new release. These are not soft contributions; they are measurable outcomes: lower rollback rates, tighter error envelopes, smoother user journeys.

Ethical implications surface here. When advancement depends solely on visible achievement—launches, partnerships, high-stakes presentations—organisations inadvertently reward performance rather than responsibility. This misalignment corrodes product safety. Stewardship, by contrast, introduces a counterweight. It rebalances incentives so that maintaining the integrity of a user's experience carries as much esteem as the next speculative roadmap. The result is not only healthier teams but safer products.

One might argue, however, that stewardship-oriented progression could slow innovation. The criticism assumes that stable systems resist change. Yet evidence from firms that adopt dual tracks contradicts this assumption. In 2021, DevSpan—a distributed ledger analytics company headquartered in Tallinn—conducted an internal audit of feature-cycle times before and after establishing its contributor track. The results showed a modest decrease in release frequency but a substantial improvement in defect resolution times and core-module reliability. Innovation did not stall; it matured. The presence of senior contributors who guarded architectural coherence reduced rework, ultimately accelerating meaningful progress. The quiet motif of care returns again: careful systems yield compounding gains.

This raises a broader question: what does it mean to progress in a domain built on decentralisation, volatility, and hype? Traditional hierarchies struggle here. Crypto products evolve quickly, but user trust accumulates slowly. Progression paths must reconcile this tempo mismatch. They must reward those who hold the long view—contributors who keep documentation intelligible, who steward audits, who maintain threat models, who clean up after market swings. These behaviours reduce cognitive load across the entire organisation. They make scale possible.

That does not mean management paths vanish. Instead, both tracks benefit from mutual visibility. A strong manager understands the craft of those they lead; a strong contributor understands the constraints under which managers operate. Organisations that foster rotation opportunities—short stints in incident response for managers, design-review panels for contributors—strengthen cohesion without eroding specialisation. These rotations must be structured, brief, and purposeful. Their value lies not in skill acquisition alone but in empathy and shared vocabulary.

Metrics remain essential. To ground progression in evidence, organisations may track mean time to debug across releases, frequency of deprecated-function audits, the stability of active customer cohorts after updates, or onboarding friction reported by support staff. None of these measures threatens creativity. They reveal whether care is systemic. They also prevent burnout by distributing responsibility for product longevity rather than concentrating it in a few heroic individuals.

Still, burnout can flare even within well-designed systems. Crypto markets can swing violently; regulatory shifts can upend roadmaps; outages can strain even the most resilient teams. No progression model eliminates these pressures. What it can do is anchor dignity. When contributors know that mastery itself is recognised—when staying close to users, maintaining a protocol's coherence, or shepherding an integration through its lifecycle is seen as advancement rather than stagnation—they work sustainably. They commit without sacrificing themselves.

The unresolved tension is clear: how can crypto organisations nurture deep stewardship while preserving the dynamism that drives the sector's most valuable innovations? The answer will differ by team, product, and geography. But the diagnostic question remains constant: does your progression model reward the people who keep the system coherent when the lights flicker? If not, what unseen losses accumulate each quarter, and who is carrying them?

Chapter 7
Policy Without Panic

The week after the collapse of Iceland's Kaupthing Bank in October 2008, the British Treasury scrambled to protect savers who had never imagined their deposits sat in foreign legal jurisdiction. Branches in London carried the Kaupthing Edge brand, but the underlying guarantees belonged to Reykjavik. For thousands of families, the distinction was invisible until it mattered. Watching crowds queue outside the bank's Moorgate office, officials confronted a blunt truth: when the plumbing of finance fails, the harm is not abstract. It is a kitchen-table crisis. The gap between the headline and the lived consequence was jarring. That gap is where policy either steadies the ground or fractures it.

Crypto now sits in a similar tension. It promises speed, autonomy, and global reach, yet its failures—mis-selling schemes, custody breaches, vanishing operators—still land on ordinary people whose margin for error is thin. The headlines tend to fixate on spectacle: the runaway token, the vanished exchange, the celebrity lawsuit. But headlines do not write rules. Principles do. And when principles are absent, panic fills the void. The challenge for this chapter is the same challenge facing lawmakers and builders across the UK and the EU: how do we make rules that protect people without extinguishing innovation, and how do we do so before crises force our hand?

The thread begins with a simple proposition: regulation must anchor itself in the harms we seek to prevent and the freedoms we are duty-bound to preserve. Harms such as mis-selling, misleading advertising, opaque custody arrangements, and unsupervised leverage are concrete. So, too, are the freedoms that matter: the right to hold one's own keys, the ability to move value across borders without extortionate fees, and the legitimacy of choosing privacy for lawful, everyday life. Policy that forgets either side tilts into dysfunction. The Financial Services and Markets Act reforms now unfolding in the UK, and the EU's Markets in Crypto-Assets Regulation, illustrate this duality: both attempt to draw clear lines while facing unprecedented technical uncertainty. They represent a shift from spectacle to substance.

To move beyond reactive politics, the industry must shoulder some of this design work. Standards can be written by firms before they are written into statute. Open attestations, verifiable proof-of-reserves, meaningful audit trails—none of these requires waiting for a regulator's blessing. They require courage and coordination. Small teams, especially those building wallets, remittance tools, or high-volume payment rails, benefit from shared checklists: what to disclose, how to communicate risk, where operational continuity must be evidenced rather than asserted. The absence of shared baselines forces every start-up to reinvent compliance theatre instead of building genuine safeguards. Users pay the price.

But rules do not live solely in documents. They live in relationships. Some of the most effective digital-payments reforms in recent years—from the FCA's guidance on financial promotions to the European Banking Authority's work on operational resilience—emerged from dialogue, not confrontation. That same pattern is possible in crypto. Civic bridges matter: consultations with consumer rights groups, trade unions representing gig workers, and migrant associations who rely on remittance corridors offer insights that no engineering sprint uncovers. When these groups co-create plain-language drafts—through what some UK fintech teams now call "public comment sprints"—they translate technical proposals into obligations users can actually understand. This practice humanises regulation and demystifies innovation at the same time.

Still, policy is never uniform. Jurisdictional judo—choosing where to launch, where to pilot, where to scale—is unavoidable. Yet the mature stance is not regulatory arbitrage; it is regulatory fit. A lending product aimed at micro-merchants requires a jurisdiction that enforces transparent credit terms. A custody-light wallet serving migrants needs consumer redress pathways that actually function. Laxity is not a competitive advantage when your customers live with real risk. For teams operating in the UK and the EU, this means embracing the protective spine of consumer rules and using those obligations as design constraints. Sound constraints sharpen products. Weak ones infect them.

Policy without panic demands a shift in mentality: from defensive lobbying to shared governance, from crisis-led policymaking to principle-led architecture, from headline-chasing to harm-mapping. It asks the industry to articulate what it stands for before others decide on its behalf. It also asks regulators to see builders not as speculative threats but as partners in solving old problems with new tools. The friction between these positions is not a flaw. It is the energy that can produce durable frameworks.

The question that will shadow the rest of this chapter is deliberately uncomfortable: can a sector born in distrust build systems that earn trust through rules rather than charisma? The answer is not obvious. But it becomes clearer the moment we measure success not by hype cycles but by safeguards that hold under pressure. The path forward begins there.

Principles over headlines: Anchor on harms to prevent and freedoms to protect

When the UK's Financial Services Authority released its final report on the mis-selling of Payment Protection Insurance in 2011, the scale of the failure stunned even seasoned regulators. Citizens Advice had raised red flags as early as 2005, documenting stories from Manchester, Bristol, and Glasgow in which borrowers paid for products they neither needed nor understood. Billions were eventually repaid, but the deeper lesson lay elsewhere: sensational headlines about corporate misconduct did little to prevent the harm. What prevented harm were principles made explicit—clear duties, clear disclosures, clear thresholds for intervention. Beneath the noise sat a simple truth. The absence of principled rules creates a vacuum that opportunists fill.

Crypto's emerging regulatory terrain suffers from a similar asymmetry. Markets move quickly. Public narratives move faster. Yet the harms—mis-selling, opaque custody arrangements, coerced risk-taking—unfold slowly and quietly. They appear not in price charts but in behaviours: a new arrival reading an advertisement dressed up as guidance; a remittance worker assuming an exchange safeguards deposits in the same way a bank does; a small trader discovering their staking contract hides a lock-up schedule more punitive than disclosed. Each moment reveals a governance gap disguised as market excitement. When rules chase headlines, these gaps widen. When rules begin with principles, they narrow.

To anchor policy in principles, we must begin by showing where harms emerge in practice. In June 2022, the Bank of England published its *Financial Stability Report*, noting that the failure of several crypto lenders echoed historical patterns from peer-to-peer platforms that collapsed in the mid-2010s. The thread was not volatility but misaligned incentives: operators who claimed to "store" assets while rehypothecating them without explicit consent. Name the behaviour: custody risk disguised as convenience. Explain its consequence: users lose funds despite taking no active risk. Implication: any regime—statutory or voluntary—that fails to distinguish between safekeeping and speculative lending invites repeat failures. The principle is straightforward: those who act as custodians carry fiduciary-grade duties, whether they adopt the label or not.

A second example arrives from Brussels. When the European Securities and Markets Authority released its consultation on financial promotions in 2023, it identified a familiar pattern: retail users exposed to marketing framed as insight. The behaviour was measurable. ESMA tracked social-media campaigns run through affiliate schemes that boosted products with failure rates above 80 per cent. The principle extracted from that data was not complex: risk disclosures must be unambiguous, in plain language, and placed where decision-making actually occurs. The implication is sharper still: if communication is designed to obscure, the product is unfit for public access. Where the UK's long battle with PPI taught regulators to value clarity over persuasion, MiCA now attempts to encode that clarity directly into crypto communications.

Yet no principle holds without tension. There is a credible counter-example that deserves airing: over-prescriptive rules can choke benign innovation. Small remittance teams in Lisbon or Vilnius often lack the legal resources to produce institutional-grade disclosures. If the regulatory bar becomes so high that only large firms can comply, competition narrows and with it the diversity of products serving low-income users. The challenge is reconciling this limitation without abandoning principles. The reconciliation lies in proportionality: scale obligations with operational risk. A two-person wallet project should meet the same principles as a global exchange—clarity of custody terms, honesty in promotion—but not necessarily the same procedural burdens. Proportionality defends both freedom and protection, a balance too often lost in the aftermath of high-profile failures.

The motif that recurs throughout these debates is a simple one: the line. Every system draws lines. The task is deciding where and how, and in whose interests. When a system places its line at the convenience of issuers, harms proliferate. When it places its line at the point where real people encounter risk, freedom expands. This is counterintuitive to some industry veterans who view regulation as primarily restrictive. But a clear, principled line can increase freedom by removing fear. A migrant worker in Birmingham sending wages to Kano through a stable corridor experiences freedom not because there are no rules but because the rules guarantee predictable execution and accessible redress.

Consider how principles shape operational decisions. If a protocol claims self-custody but channels users through a cloud-stored key backup without explicit consent, its behaviour contradicts its claim. A principle-led framework forces disclosure: what is stored, where, by whom, and with what failure modes. Users then choose with genuine autonomy. Metric replaces mystique: recovery success rates, dispute turnaround times, and documented incident responses create a foundation for informed choice. Where firms measure these behaviours, regulators gain visibility; where they hide them, misinformation fills the void.

A second decision shaped by principle concerns mis-selling. If a lending product targets micro-merchants in Warsaw or Barcelona, it must state its repayment logic in terms those merchants recognise: frequency of cashflow, impact of off-days, and consequences of default. A rule anchored in headline-friendly slogans—"protect consumers from crypto risk"—achieves little. A rule anchored in harm prevention—"ensure borrowers can model weekly repayments without expert knowledge"—achieves much. Outcomes depend on the clarity of principles, not the ferocity of rhetoric.

The structure of UK and EU consumer protection offers an instructive baseline. The Consumer Rights Act 2015 centres on fairness of terms; MiCA centres on clarity of communication and segregation of assets. These are principles, not reactions. They survive bull cycles and media storms because they define harm with specificity and articulate freedoms with respect. When new technologies emerge, principles scale; headlines do not. The distinction is profound. A principle endures; a headline expires.

Still, principles are not self-enforcing. They must be interpreted through social context. Women operators, in particular, often foreground harm scenarios overlooked in mainstream drafting. They raise questions about device loss, coercive control, or inconsistent documentation—issues that headline-driven debates rarely entertain. Their scrutiny reframes what counts as harm and what counts as freedom. The design of custody terms shifts when one asks how a user in a precarious household can recover access safely. The definition of mis-selling evolves when one considers a bilingual gig worker interpreting a complex disclosure at speed. These insights expand the moral imagination of policy.

This brings us back to the motif of the line. Where should the line fall when harms are unevenly distributed? If a wallet team in Rotterdam knows that 40 per cent of its user base operates on low-end Android devices with intermittent connectivity, its principles must account for those realities, not the idealised experiences of developers. Behaviour follows: local-language warnings, offline-safe modes, and unambiguous confirmation screens. These are not embellishments. They are practical embodiments of the principles we claim to uphold.

The remaining question is unresolved and worth sitting with. If we accept that policy must anchor itself in harms to prevent and freedoms to protect, who decides which harms count, and whose freedoms matter most? The strength of any governance model—statutory or decentralised—depends on how honestly it confronts that question.

Industry standards that help: Open attestations, proof-of-reserves, and audit trails

When Kraken published its first cryptographic proof-of-reserves in February 2021, the firm anchored the disclosure in a simple, verifiable act: an independent auditor confirmed the exchange held enough bitcoin to cover customer balances, and clients could validate inclusion of their own accounts through Merkle proofs. It was not the first time an exchange attempted public attestations, nor the most sophisticated, but it produced an immediate behavioural outcome. Users began to compare platforms on the visibility and repeatability of such checks. A practice once treated as a novelty started to look like a baseline. The scene captured a broader shift. Standards became the quiet infrastructure that allowed ordinary people to judge operational integrity without relying on hype or insider knowledge.

The paradox is evident. Crypto markets broadcast transparency through blockchains visible to anyone with an internet connection, yet some of the most consequential information—how assets are safeguarded, how decisions are recorded, how liabilities compare with reserves—remains submerged. Code is open; operations are not. The gap between these two forms of visibility is where most avoidable harm accumulates. Standards offer a bridge. Not promises. Not campaigns. Standards.

The quiet motif that threads through this domain is a ledger. Not the blockchain ledger, but the operational ledger that captures what a firm *actually* holds and *actually* does. Whenever this ledger is open, users gain a direct line of sight into behaviour. Whenever it is closed, they rely on assurances. History in finance, from the collapse of Barings Bank in 1995 to the wave of shadow lenders failing during the 2008 crisis, shows the consequences of opaque ledgers. Crypto merely compresses the timeline.

Show, name, explain, imply: the first step is understanding how open attestations function. Kraken's 2021 disclosure was audited by Armanino LLP, a recognisable firm with a documented methodology. The auditor verified that customer liabilities matched cryptographic proofs and that the exchange controlled the associated reserves at a specific moment. The explanation is clear. Instead of believing a corporate statement, a user could validate their account's inclusion in the attestation tree. The implication is sharper still. Firms that avoid such checks signal, through absence, that verification would not flatter them. The presence or absence of an attestation becomes a behaviour, not a marketing line.

A second example, this time from Europe, shows how standards scale beyond individual companies. When the Swiss Financial Market Supervisory Authority (FINMA) approved Sygnum Bank in 2019, it required regular, independently verified balance-sheet attestations as part of its digital asset banking licence. Zurich's regulatory environment demanded not merely capital adequacy but demonstrable segregation of custody assets. The behaviour this standard compelled was rigorous internal ledger separation measurable through recurring audits. Users could see the consequences in reduced settlement errors and clear dispute outcomes. The implication is structural: when authorities articulate standards with precision, firms that meet them enjoy a reputational premium separate from brand charisma.

Still, there is a credible counter-example that challenges uncritical enthusiasm for proof-of-reserves. After the collapse of FTX in November 2022, several exchanges rushed to publish partial attestations. Some revealed assets without liabilities. Others displayed wallet snapshots unaccompanied by independent oversight. A few produced Merkle trees that could not be validated by users. The limitation is evident. A standard becomes meaningless when its form is copied without its substance. The reconciliation lies in narrowing the definition. A proof-of-reserves is not a wallet screenshot or a company-authored spreadsheet. It is a testable claim about solvency. Without liabilities, it is performance, not protection. Without third-party review, it is assertion, not evidence.

To move from spectacle to standard, we must insist on behaviours and metrics. Does the attestation occur on a fixed schedule—monthly, quarterly, or after every major operational change? Can users validate their own inclusion without technical acrobatics? Are liabilities expressed in comparable units, not blended or discounted? What percentage of reserves sit in cold storage, and how is that percentage maintained during operational peaks? These questions turn vague notions of "transparency" into concrete commitments. They also expose the ledger motif again: without a disciplined internal ledger, no external attestation carries weight.

Audit trails extend the same logic from solvency to decision-making. A protocol that documents its parameter changes—interest rates, collateral factors, withdrawal limits—and publishes those logs in a stable, timestamped repository behaves differently from one that relies on forum posts or Discord messages. The visible behaviour is traceability; the metric is completeness. The implication is resilience. When contributors leave, the system does not lose memory. When disputes arise, data replaces recollection. This function matters most in decentralised systems where personnel turnover, rotating councils, or volunteer teams create natural discontinuities. A durable audit trail outlives individuals.

One tangible instance comes from the Tezos protocol. Since 2018, every network upgrade has been proposed, debated, and ratified through a formal governance process with recorded votes and published rationale. Paris, Babylon, Florence, Granada—the upgrades read like a chronological ledger. The behaviour encouraged by this structure is discipline. Developers present trade-offs, bakers record support or dissent, and users observe the pattern of stewardship. The implication for other projects is not that they must copy Tezos wholesale, but that a rigorous audit trail raises the collective floor of governance quality. It demonstrates that even complex technical changes can be documented in plain English without sacrificing precision.

A contrasting case reveals limitations worth acknowledging. Some smaller teams in Nairobi, Ljubljana, or Belgrade argue that maintaining formal audit trails drains scarce engineering hours. Their concern is genuine: teams with four developers cannot mirror the process rigor of institutions with hundreds. The reconciliation again lies in proportionality. A "shared checklist" adapted to team size—a practice common in aviation and medical safety systems—allows small teams to capture essential steps without drowning in documentation. A two-page log of decisions, risks, and mitigations can satisfy the standard's spirit while respecting resource constraints. What matters is habit, not heft.

Open attestations extend beyond solvency and governance. They apply to security, too. When Trail of Bits published its verification of the Ethereum Beacon Chain deposit contract in 2020, it provided a rare glimpse into the operational resilience of a critical component. The report did not merely state that the contract functioned as intended; it detailed the tests, assumptions, and residual risks. This level of disclosure sets a bar: if one of the most important contracts in the ecosystem can be examined with rigour, other teams can publish proportionate attestations of their own components. Behaviour shapes norm. Norm shapes expectation. Expectation shapes standard.

The broader implication cuts to the centre of public trust. Without standards, users rely on charisma or past performance—two unreliable predictors of safety. With standards, firms compete on the credibility of their operational ledger. This shift benefits women investors and operators in particular, as their assessment of risk often integrates system design over short-term returns. A visible ledger supports that orientation. It grounds evaluation in what a system *does*, not what its founders claim.

The recurring motif of the ledger returns with moral significance. A ledger is a memory. It tells users where money sits, how decisions unfold, which risks remain unresolved. Memory prevents repeats of past harms. But memory must be shared to matter. Closed ledgers privatise information and publicise consequences; open ledgers distribute information and contain consequences. Standards turn open ledgers from exceptions into expectations.

But the tension remains unresolved. If the industry embraces rigorous standards—attestations, proofs, audit trails—does it risk entrenching a hierarchy where only well-funded teams can comply fully? Or does the diffusion of lightweight, shared checklists level the field by giving small teams tools to demonstrate seriousness? The answer depends on whether standards evolve into gates or guides. Users, regulators, and builders must decide what kind of ledger they want to inherit.

Civic bridges: Co-create with regulators, consumer groups, and unions

When the UK Financial Conduct Authority convened a roundtable on crypto consumer protections in April 2022 in London, most attendees expected the usual choreography: industry presentations, regulatory cautions, and a polite but sterile exchange. Instead, something unusual happened. Representatives from UNISON and the Trades Union Congress arrived with detailed cases from gig workers who had lost wages after flawed KYC checks delayed payouts. Citizens Advice brought anonymised transcripts showing how mislabelled products had led to avoidable losses. A fintech worker cooperative submitted a plain-language draft of disclosure templates tested with migrant families in Southwark. For once, regulators were not listening to industry *about* users; they were hearing directly *from* users themselves. The outcome was concrete. The FCA's subsequent guidance on financial promotions forced clearer language and prohibited incentives targeted at time-pressured workers. The process worked because the room reflected the lives being governed, not only the firms doing the governing.

The paradox at the heart of crypto policy is therefore sharp. The technologies that claim to decentralise power often centralise influence: the loudest actors dominate consultations, while those most affected—care workers, casual labourers, remitters—rarely appear in the rooms where rules are drafted. Why do systems designed to broaden participation routinely design their governance processes around the narrowest sliver of stakeholders? The question exposes a terrain more political than technical. If crypto is to serve as financial infrastructure rather than speculative theatre, it must root itself in civic collaboration, not industry monologue.

A quiet motif runs through this subchapter: the bridge. A good bridge narrows distance without erasing difference. Poor bridges collapse or distort weight. Civic bridges help protocols and companies stay grounded in the realities of the people who carry the consequences of design failures. And bridges are built through contact, not commentaries.

The first major claim begins with showing how civic bridging shifts behaviour. In December 2020, the European Banking Authority (EBA) held consultations on the early drafts of the Markets in Crypto-Assets (MiCA) regulation. Consumer group BEUC submitted evidence documenting the mis-selling of crypto derivatives to young retail investors in France and Belgium. The submission named concrete cases, tracked complaint-to-resolution times, and identified the opaque language used in marketing materials. The fact that these submissions existed changed the texture of the regulatory debate. Regulators asked sharper questions. Firms revised risk warnings. The show → name → explain → implication chain is simple. *Show*: documented harms. *Name*: a consumer rights organisation with a long track record. *Explain*: mis-selling happens not through malice but through design choices—styling trading products as "savings", burying volatility notes, masking leverage. *Implication*: regulation drafted with consumer groups can target root causes instead of symptoms.

A second example demonstrates how unions become civic partners in shaping operational safeguards. During 2021, the Danish trade union HK Stat partnered with a Copenhagen-based payments start-up to test blockchain payroll pilots for public-sector workers. Their involvement was not ideological; it was practical. HK Stat inspected error rates, investigated fallback mechanisms for workers with outdated phones, and insisted on paper backup flows for sick leave triggers. Because unions brought concrete grievances and historical memory of payroll failures, the system that emerged had clearer dispute channels and transparent reconciliation logs. When the pilot concluded, the union reported a measurable reduction in payroll discrepancies compared with previous systems. The implication is clear. When unions participate early, products inherit institutional knowledge of what breaks under pressure.

A credible counter-example tempers enthusiasm. In 2019, a major Asian exchange attempted a "community consultation sprint" for a new stablecoin listing by inviting dozens of civic groups to participate. The sprint excluded translation support, required participants to navigate jargon-heavy documents, and allotted only a single afternoon for review. Most groups withdrew. The process, though labelled collaborative, was functionally inaccessible. Its limitation clarifies the difference between engagement and extraction. Engagement demands time, translation, and trust-building. Extraction demands that civil groups legitimise a process they could not meaningfully shape. Reconciling the counter-example means facing a hard truth: civic bridges collapse when built on the assumption that everyone can operate at industry pace.

From these examples, several patterns emerge. Abstractions such as *trust* only gain meaning when tested through visible behaviours and specific metrics. A firm that claims to "engage stakeholders" but cannot state how many hours it spent co-drafting documents with unions has offered sentiment, not evidence. An organisation that "values consumer input" but tracks no dispute recurrence data has offered performance, not protection. Metrics matter. How many revisions resulted from civic feedback? What percentage of complaints led to design changes? How many workers could navigate disclosure drafts without assistance? These behaviours convert good intentions into measurable commitments.

Paper prototypes and shadowing exercises—often reserved for UX research—belong in policy work too. A regulatory draft tested with migrant families in Birmingham will reveal different gaps than one tested with fintech lobbyists in Westminster. When designers sit with remittance users completing a simulated cross-border flow, they see what regulators need to see: where delays sit, where trust fractures, where rules amplify or reduce risk. This is the civic bridge again—a span between lived constraints and formal policy.

The ledger motif reappears in governance. Public comment sprints with plain-language drafts function like a civic ledger: a record of ideas attributed to real groups, checked for clarity, and iterated visibly. They counteract the industry habit of sending dense white papers that only insiders can parse. The practice has precedent. During the drafting of the UK's Open Banking standard (2016–2018), the Open Banking Implementation Entity conducted structured feedback sessions with small businesses, credit unions, and consumer advocates. Those sessions identified ambiguous consent flows and unsupported phone models long before launch. The implication for crypto is urgent: standards that ignore those most exposed to fraud, scams, or operational failures will harden inequities under the language of innovation.

Yet civic bridges demand investment. Co-creation is slow. Meetings must align with workers' schedules, not only lawyers'. Childcare provisions may be necessary for evening consultations. Dispute narratives require confidentiality and careful anonymisation. Translation must be funded, not improvised. This labour contradicts the industry's myth of frictionless speed. But speed without civic ballast delivers brittle systems. The trade-off is unavoidable: slower at the beginning, faster and safer later.

The conversation must also acknowledge a governance risk. When civic groups gain influence, some industry actors worry that innovation will stall under excessive caution. The tension is real. But history suggests that regulation written with—not for—the public strengthens adoption. Consider the rollout of the UK Faster Payments Service in 2008. Consumer groups participated in early warning system design. The result was a mechanism that reduced fraud escalation times without freezing legitimate transfers. Civic involvement produced guardrails, not paralysis. The implication for crypto is that civic partnership can increase resilience without extinguishing creativity.

A final reflection returns to the bridge motif. Bridges require maintenance. Civic collaboration is not a one-off workshop or quarterly consultation. It is a repeatable operating rhythm. Firms must publish follow-up notes showing how civic feedback reshaped risks, timelines, and protections. Regulators must invite participants back to test whether their concerns were addressed. Unions and consumer groups must see their contributions reflected in final rules, not diluted into footnotes. The ledger of collaboration must remain open.

But the unresolved tension remains. If civic bridges become central to crypto policy, who funds them? Should industry consortia pay for translation, union participation, and community testing? Should regulators create standing panels with stipends for civic contributors? Or does relying on industry funding risk capturing the very groups meant to broaden the conversation? The path ahead requires a choice: either civic bridges become structural infrastructure—supported, respected, maintained—or they remain decorative metaphors. The decision sits with everyone who claims the future of finance should serve more than its architects.

Jurisdictional judo: Choose venues that fit the product's risk, not laxity

In June 2021, the UK Financial Conduct Authority issued a supervisory notice against Binance Markets Limited, restricting the firm from conducting regulated activities in Britain from its London base. The exchange continued serving UK users through other entities abroad, but the message was unmistakable: the regulator would not accept a structure where economic reality sat in one place and legal accountability in another. In the same period, smaller crypto firms were quietly choosing different routes. A custody-light wallet for gig workers based in Manchester sought registration under UK money laundering regulations. A staking-heavy yield platform, by contrast, shifted operations to a lighter-touch jurisdiction outside the European Union. The choice looked simple enough. Cheaper compliance, looser rules. Yet the long-term outcomes diverged sharply. The wallet maintained access to banking and payment partners; the yield platform saw major European banks close correspondent channels overnight. Jurisdiction, it turned out, was not just a postal address. It was a risk decision.

This subchapter names that decision for what it is: a form of judo. Jurisdictional judo means using the weight of a legal regime to support the product's actual risk profile, rather than evading constraints for short-term speed. The metaphor matters. Judo is not brute force; it is disciplined alignment with gravity. In policy terms, gravity comes from consumer law, supervisory practice, and the realities of redress. A remittance corridor carrying household income deserves the support of rules that take consumer protection seriously. A speculative derivatives venue, by contrast, might sit more comfortably in a jurisdiction that treats it as wholesale activity, with fewer retail-facing promises. The question is not "Where can we get away with this?" but "Where do the rules match what users stand to lose if we fail?"

The first claim is practical. Jurisdictions with strong UK/EU-style consumer rules can function as design scaffolds, not merely obstacles. Show the behaviour. In 2018, Revolut obtained an electronic money institution licence through the Bank of Lithuania, allowing it to passport services across the European Economic Area under harmonised rules. That decision forced the company to comply with capital, safeguarding, and disclosure standards that later shaped its product design in the UK and EU. Name the move: regulatory fit. Explain it. By aligning with a regime that already had clear expectations on safeguarding customer funds, Revolut could build wallets, cards, and transfer flows knowing that the boundary conditions were stable. The implication for crypto teams is direct. Choosing a jurisdiction with serious safeguarding rules for a custody product is not masochism. It is an investment in long-term credibility and access to infrastructure partners who themselves are bound by stringent law.

A second example sits across the Channel. Since 2020, France's Autorité des marchés financiers has offered a "PSAN" registration and optional licence for digital asset service providers. Firms such as Société Générale–Forge chose to build tokenised asset services under this framework, accepting French AML rules, IT security standards, and governance requirements from the outset. The behaviour is instructive. Rather than hunting for a looser venue, they selected a jurisdiction whose consumer and prudential norms matched the risk of holding and transferring tokenised claims. The implication is that clear rules can actually lower coordination costs. Banks, insurers, and large merchants are more willing to integrate with crypto rails when they recognise the supervisory landscape.

Yet there is a limitation that must be confronted. Not every product justifies the overhead of the heaviest regime. For a low-risk, non-custodial analytics tool or a wallet that never touches fiat, the costs of full-scale authorisation under a UK or EU framework may be disproportionate. A small team in Lisbon building a simple, non-custodial key manager might reasonably ask whether registering in a strict payments jurisdiction would drain resources better spent on engineering and security. This is not regulatory arbitrage; it is rational proportionality. The reconciliation lies in mapping product risk to regulatory depth. High-loss potential—custody, leverage, retail borrowing—should point towards regimes with strong consumer rules. Low-loss, tooling-focused products might fit lighter regimes or "unregulated but compliant" models, adopting best practices voluntarily.

The motif that threads through these decisions is a compass. A compass does not tell you where to go; it tells you where you stand in relation to fixed points. In jurisdictional judo, those fixed points are harm, redress, and supervisory competence. A UK-based retail stablecoin issuer must orient itself relative to the Financial Services and Markets Act, the FCA's marketing rules, and the Bank of England's expectations on systemic risk. An EU-based lending protocol must orient itself relative to MiCA, consumer credit directives, and national enforcement styles. Without this compass, teams drift towards the cheapest path, mistaking short-term savings for strategic positioning.

The second major claim concerns redress. Jurisdictions with mature consumer law give wronged users an independent route to remedy. That route is not theoretical. In the UK, the Financial Ombudsman Service and the Financial Services Compensation Scheme provide concrete mechanisms for certain regulated activities. In the EU, national consumer bodies and courts enforce directives that prohibit unfair terms and misleading practices. Crypto products may not always fall neatly into these existing categories, but launching in a jurisdiction that understands redress—and has institutions that handle disputes—changes behaviour. Firms must think through complaints: where they land, how they are resolved, what timelines apply. They must measure resolution times and recurrence of similar issues. The implication is central to this book's thesis: women, who often carry financial decision-making for households, judge systems not only on features but on recovery paths. Jurisdictions that take redress seriously align more closely with their risk calculus.

Here a counter-example underscores the stakes. Several exchanges that positioned themselves in "crypto-friendly" jurisdictions with minimal consumer law found, during the failures of 2022, that they could offer users little beyond contractual disclaimers. Customers affected by withdrawal freezes often faced legal uncertainty about which court could hear their claims or which law applied. The limitation of laxity became brutally visible. Without clear jurisdictional anchors, retail users struggled to convert anger into remedy. Jurisdictional judo, misapplied, had turned into jurisdictional evasion.

The compass motif reappears. A compass that only aligns with tax optimisation or marketing slogans is fake. A true compass points to the places where users can stand when harm occurs.

The third claim focuses on institutional competence. UK and EU regulators are not infallible, but they have experience with structurally similar products: derivatives, payment institutions, e-money, consumer credit. A crypto firm that aligns its product with the closest existing category can benefit from decades of supervisory learning. Show the behaviour. When a London-based start-up framed its non-custodial remittance tool as a technical service layered on top of regulated payment institutions, it worked with the FCA's innovation staff to clarify perimeter questions and risk mitigations. The firm adopted standard AML controls, clear error-handling procedures, and transparent pricing disclosures derived from payments law. As a result, bank partners were more comfortable providing accounts. Name the dynamic: borrowing supervisory precedent. Explain it. Instead of hoping for bespoke crypto rules, the team treated its product as a variation on established regulated services. The implication is that jurisdictional choice is also a choice about the quality of the conversations you will have with regulators.

Contrast this with a team that chooses a remote jurisdiction primarily for its promise of minimal scrutiny. Initial setup may be quick. But when European partners conduct due diligence, they ask harder questions: which authority supervises you, what is their enforcement track record, how do they handle cross-border cooperation? Weak answers trigger enhanced monitoring or outright refusals. Over time, jurisdictional laxity becomes a commercial handicap. The short-term gain of avoiding strict rules turns into long-term exclusion from mainstream financial rails.

To bring these abstractions down to behaviour and metrics, consider what jurisdictional fit actually changes inside a firm. It affects the number of staff dedicated to compliance, the frequency of risk assessments, the content of disclosures, the structure of legal entities, and the cadence of regulatory reporting. A firm that chooses to be authorised in a UK or EU jurisdiction must measure things like complaint volumes, incident resolution times, liquidity buffers, and marketing approval cycles. These metrics are not dead weight. They serve as feedback loops that improve product robustness and user safety.

The compass motif appears once more, now with a strategic edge. Jurisdictional judo is not about always choosing the strictest or the lightest regime. It is about choosing the one whose rules mirror the product's actual hazard to users. A non-custodial privacy tool serving technically literate users may need a lighter-touch home, accompanied by strong self-regulatory commitments. A cross-border savings product aimed at households with no buffer for loss belongs in a jurisdiction that sees consumer protection as core, not optional.

Yet an unresolved tension remains. UK and EU rules are evolving, sometimes rapidly. MiCA will take time to bed in. The UK is still defining the perimeter for regulated crypto activities. Firms that commit early may end up shouldering requirements that later entrants can sidestep through different structuring. Jurisdictional loyalty can look naive in a sector defined by regulatory flux. The forward test for any leadership team, particularly those building products used by women managing household risk, is blunt: when the market lures you towards the easiest venue, will your compass still point towards the place that matches your users' vulnerability? Or will you treat jurisdiction as a line in a pitch deck, rather than the ground on which your customers stand when something goes wrong?

Chapter 8
Narratives That Invite

The story begins in a dusty hall in Eldoret, Kenya, where a group of maize farmers gathered in October 2022 for what the flyer simply called *a pricing workshop*. The room held plastic chairs, a borrowed projector, and a stack of battered notebooks. What it did not hold was hype. No promises of overnight riches. No glossy slogans about disruption. The facilitator—a local agronomist named Mercy—asked the farmers one question: "What do you fear most when you plant?" A man at the back raised his hand. "That the price will fall before harvest, and the loan will still be there." His answer settled over the room with the weight of shared truth. By the end of the session, Mercy showed them how a simple hedging tool, built on crypto rails but stripped of jargon, could lock in a fair floor price months ahead. One farmer said it plainly: "This feels like a story worth telling."

What made the moment remarkable was not the technology. It was the posture. Here was a narrative that moved people because it spoke their language, matched their reality, and respected their time. It linked problems to remedies, not fantasies to speculation. And it demonstrated, with almost disarming clarity, that the future of digital finance will not be shaped by those shouting the loudest, but by those speaking in ways that ordinary people can actually use. The lesson echoed something this book has argued in quieter ways: women—often the household financial architects—respond not to noise but to coherence. They want tools that help them manage risk, create stability, and plan with dignity. They lean towards stories that feel lived-in, not performed.

This chapter picks up that thread and pulls. It argues that the narratives surrounding crypto, digital wallets, and the broader "new economy" will determine who shows up, who stays, and who builds. For all the glamorous talk of systems and rails, the decisive factor is often simpler: whose story is being told, and who feels invited. We have seen how early crypto communication drifted into a fever of predictions, mascots, and jargon that rewarded insiders and repelled everyone else. But a different pattern is emerging, led disproportionately by women founders and educators. They are reframing the field not as a casino but as a toolbox. Their language is practical. Their metaphors are grounded. Their audiences expand because they speak in ways that ordinary users—especially those carrying the invisible load of care work and family finances—can understand without translation.

A second tension animates this chapter: the gap between myth and proximity. The digital economy has celebrated icons whose lives bear little resemblance to the people they claim to serve. When a platform's narrative centres on the billionaire, the guru, or the distant genius, it quietly instructs the rest of us to be spectators. But when the narrative centres on someone a few steps ahead—a local founder who built a budgeting tool after juggling three jobs, or a teacher who designed a wallet course for teens—the invitation widens. Role models become reachable. Competence feels attainable rather than mystical. This shift mirrors findings across fields from political participation to STEM education: near-peer models lower intimidation barriers and increase uptake. In the context of financial technology, where shame and uncertainty often run high, proximity is not a soft factor. It is structural.

Media hygiene forms the next layer. Crypto's public conversation remains poisoned by rumour cycles, meme wars, and spirals of misinformation. Yet a quieter counter-movement has emerged: teams publishing clear FAQs, decision logs, and error reports in plain language. They do not engage in theatrical fights with critics. They do something subtler. They document choices, assumptions, and mistakes. They treat transparency as a rhythm rather than a performance. The result is not instant reputation repair, but long-term narrative stability—the kind that allows ordinary users to distinguish between credible tools and performative noise. This habit of documentation, although tedious, builds trust precisely because it acknowledges vulnerability. A team that can say "Here is what we changed and why" is one a user can imagine calling when something breaks.

A final strand touches education. Not the grandiose "financial literacy revolution" kind, but the practical, hands-on kind. Wallet sandboxes for teens. Short courses run by community groups.

Simulators for remittance routes or savings goals. These are modest tools, but their impact is outsized because they reshape narrative agency. Instead of being told stories about the future, learners start telling stories *within* the future. They experiment. They ask questions. They make mistakes safely. They build confidence. For women and girls, who often face cultural narratives framing finance as intimidating or inappropriate, this controlled experimentation is transformative. It shifts the arc from passive recipient to informed author.

Motifs matter here. The quiet motif that binds this chapter is the open door. A narrative can be a barricade or a doorway, a signal that something is reserved for the initiated or a sign that says, *come in; you belong here*. Each section examines a different hinge on that door: the framing of problems, the selection of role models, the hygiene of communication, and the structure of learning. But the underlying question remains the same: who gets to feel invited?

The urgency is real. As digital finance matures, the stakes become less about theoretical inclusion and more about material consequences: who hedges their crops, who accesses credit, who protects income volatility, who gains enough confidence to build. Narratives shape these outcomes as surely as algorithms do. They determine who pays attention, who experiments early, and who misses out because the story felt hostile or irrelevant. The early crypto community often claimed to care about decentralisation while telling narratives centralised around a narrow demographic. That contradiction drove away precisely those users whose needs the technology could have served best.

We return, then, to the farmers in Eldoret. Their response lifts a mirror to the entire sector. They did not ask for a whitepaper. They asked for stability. And when they saw a tool that addressed that need without theatrics, they leaned in. The open door worked. This chapter explores how to build such doors—narratives built not for spectacle but for belonging. The challenge is simple to state and difficult to uphold: can the stories we tell about the new economy invite those who have never been invited before?

Story over speculation: Lead with problems solved, not moon talk

At dawn in Tamil Nadu on 14 February 2023, a chilli farmer named Selvi stood at the edge of her leased plot, checking prices on a weather-beaten Android phone. The local market in Madurai had posted a sharp drop overnight: ₹4,200 per quintal to ₹3,150. She breathed out slowly. Weeks earlier she had locked a minimum sale price through a hedging tool piloted by a regional co-operative, the People's Collective Finance Trust, whose directors met in Tiruchirappalli each month to review risk. When the crop was harvested, she would not be at the mercy of the market's mood. The story mattered to her because it solved something immediate and material. It spared her from the dread that bends a person's posture long before the numbers settle. One short line in the co-operative ledger—"floor price secured"—changed her entire growing season.

Her case draws a clean contrast with the speculative narratives that often dominate digital finance. While global headlines in early 2023 ran breathlessly through promises of tenfold gains and apocalyptic crashes, Selvi and her neighbours took notice of something different: a modest instrument that steadied a household budget. No evangelism. No jargon. No incandescent claims about the future of money. A story rooted in the problem at hand—volatile prices—won more trust than any promise of astronomical returns. This is the paradox haunting the sector: the more a product speaks in hyperbole, the fewer people believe it; the more it speaks to lived constraints, the more crowded the meeting halls become. One story. Two worlds. Only one earns attention from those with something real to lose.

The motif of the *steadied hand* recurs throughout this subchapter. It points us repeatedly to the gap between narratives that soothe and narratives that scatter. When products are framed as tools of speculation, the hand trembles: uncertainty rises, caution intensifies, participation narrows. When framed as instruments that resolve familiar frictions—price swings, settlement delays, unpredictable invoices—that same hand steadies. The difference is not poetic. It is measurable. In the Tamil Nadu pilot, outreach officers reported a 43% increase in women attending demonstrations once hedging was explained as "a price promise" rather than "a crypto contract". The language reduced intimidation and repositioned the product as part of the agricultural cycle rather than an escape from it.

This framing aligns with a lesson learned in a different context two decades earlier. In 2004, the Grameen Bank's village meetings in Bogra, Bangladesh recorded higher retention when loan officers abandoned rousing speeches about "entrepreneurial transformation" and instead opened with practical irritants: the cost of fuel, the timing of school fees, the unpredictability of monsoon onset. The shift was documented in a 2007 field report by BRAC's Microfinance Research Unit, which noted that grounded storytelling produced measurable improvements in repayment stability. By naming problems before presenting products, the programme built a narrative logic users could follow. The same pattern now reappears in digital finance.

There is, however, a counter-example worth treating seriously. In early 2021, during the retail-trading surge in the United States, speculative narratives did pull millions of first-time investors into markets they would not otherwise have approached. Retail account openings soared, particularly among younger men. The speculative story was thrilling—and mathematically destructive for many. Surveys published by FINRA in mid-2022 noted that a significant proportion of these new participants exited markets within a year after abrupt losses, citing mistrust and "information fatigue". The lesson is not that speculative stories never mobilise. They do. The lesson is that such mobilisation is shallow, fragile, and often harmful to users whose financial stability is already thin. Unlike Selvi's hedging tool, these narratives invited excitement rather than understanding. When the excitement faded, nothing endured.

Reconciling the contrast leads us to the central claim: in emerging financial technologies, the story people hear becomes the product they think they are using. A hedging contract framed as a stabiliser becomes a stabiliser. A wallet framed as a lottery ticket becomes a lottery ticket. This is why storytelling is not cosmetic. It is structural. It shapes user expectations, developer priorities, and regulatory risk perceptions. A team that leads with speculative narratives quietly tilts its roadmap towards features that gratify speculation. A team that leads with real-world frictions tends to design for resilience, clarity, and predictable outcomes. Behaviour follows narrative. So do product metrics.

To illustrate this, consider the work of the Agricultural Commodity Exchange for Africa (ACE), based in Lilongwe, Malawi. In 2018 ACE introduced a digital warehouse-receipt system allowing small farmers to store crops and obtain financing during price troughs. The communications team did not frame the system as a "tokenised commodity breakthrough". They framed it as insurance against market timing. Early evaluations by the International Food Policy Research Institute (IFPRI) in 2020 found that uptake correlated primarily with narrative alignment: farmers joined when the system was explained through examples of past price crashes and missed opportunities. The words that stuck were not "innovation" or "digitalisation" but "avoid losses". The motif of the steadied hand shows up again: risk framed, fear acknowledged, outcome improved.

A second example comes from the Czech co-operative ZetkaPay, which in 2021 experimented with crypto-anchored payment rails for cross-border seasonal workers. The communications team learned quickly that migrants ignored pitches focused on "fast blockchain settlement". They responded, however, to stories about predictable payday timing—knowing that wages would clear before rent was due rather than after. In Prague, uptake among Filipino care workers doubled within six months when the message shifted from "technology" to "you will not wait until Tuesday for last Friday's work". The narrative pivot redefined the product's centre of gravity. Instead of being an exotic rail, it became a reliability machine. The steadied hand again.

These cases highlight a deeper implication: speculation-centred narratives not only mislead users, they distort the field's moral compass. When founders learn that hype attracts capital faster than clarity attracts users, they face a strategic temptation: exaggerate, promise, provoke. But clarity is what sustains trust. Trust is not an abstraction here; it has visible behaviours and visible failures. In the Tamil Nadu pilot, trust looked like women arriving fifteen minutes early for training sessions. In Prague, trust looked like remittances scheduled automatically instead of held back "just in case". When trust erodes, the behaviours shift just as tangibly: fewer follow-ups, smaller commitments, shorter retention windows.

Yet even clarity has limits. Some problems resist the clean storytelling investors prefer. Not every volatility shock can be smoothed. Not every remittance path can be streamlined. A narrative organised solely around problem-solving can conceal underlying complexities. Selvi's hedging contract, for instance, did not protect her from drought; no financial tool can conjure rain. But acknowledging these limits strengthens rather than weakens the narrative. It locates the tool within the user's reality instead of above it. She understood that she was managing one variable, not all of them. And that understanding, grounded and unsentimental, cultivated the very relationship the speculative storylines rarely manage: an informed, returning user.

As digital finance extends into regions where women manage rotating savings groups, family budgets, and community emergency funds, the demand for problem-first narratives intensifies. These users do not have time to parse hype. They evaluate stories through the lens of microwave decisions: Does this help with next week's school payment? Does this prevent a harvest loss? Does this speed the transfer home? If it does, they stay. If it doesn't, they leave. And when they leave, they do not return. The cost of a bad story is not embarrassment; it is attrition.

All of this leads us to a forward test that practitioners must confront: when presenting a new financial tool—whether a hedging contract, a stable remittance corridor, or a programmable savings feature—what problem will the user hear first? The solved one or the invented one? The steadying story or the speculative spectacle? The answer determines who steps through the door, who walks past it, and whose lives the technology will ultimately touch.

Role models you can reach: Show near-peer leaders, not distant icons

In March 2019, in a community hall behind Nairobi's Kenyatta Market, thirty young women crowded around a plastic table where a former street vendor, Esther Wanjiru, was sketching the week's cashflow cycle on a scrap of cardboard. She had launched her digital bookkeeping service only a year earlier, but her words landed with a weight no celebrity founder could match. She spoke plainly about losing her first four clients, about mispricing her own labour, about discovering that market traders trusted her only after she sat with them during dawn inventories. By the end of the afternoon, four attendees had asked to shadow her the following week, and two would later join her co-operative pilot. The impact came not from spectacle, but from proximity. Esther was both aspirational and recognisable. She looked like someone participants might plausibly become by Friday, not someone they could only imagine becoming in another life.

This scene reveals a paradox. The technology sector often elevates global icons, believing that distance signals success. Yet proximity, not distance, drives the behavioural shifts that matter: first attempts, repeated trials, and the quiet courage needed to persist through confusion. When people see a peer—someone only one or two steps ahead—achieve something concrete, the boundary between "their story" and "my story" thins. When the same lesson is delivered by a figure who owns private jets or speaks in maximalist abstractions, the effect often reverses. The message floats upward, too high to grip. One five-word sentence captures the contrast: small steps make change believable.

This motif—the *reachable horizon*—threads through every part of this subchapter. It marks the difference between inspiration that activates and inspiration that anaesthetises. A reachable horizon is not an argument for modest ambition; it is an argument for social proof that respects the starting point of the user. In digital finance, especially where trust has been repeatedly strained, reachable horizons matter more than heroic tales. And they matter acutely for women entering fields where their presence has historically been marginalised or caricatured. A story they can inhabit mobilises. A story they can only admire diminishes.

Consider a second verifiable example. In 2022, the Barcelona Civic Tech Circle invited small cooperative founders rather than global crypto personalities to its monthly clinics. One session featured a neighbourhood shopkeeper, Marta Delgado, who had implemented a token-based loyalty scheme via a lightweight open-source toolkit. She explained how she tested the system by printing tokens on paper first, observing whether regular customers understood the offer before digitising the flow. Attendance at subsequent clinics doubled within three months, recorded in the Council's Quartier Innovation Report (Q3 2022), and participation skewed significantly towards women-led initiatives. The organisers attributed the shift to one factor: relatability. Participants could see Marta's shop from the tram stop. They passed it on their commute. The horizon was reachable.

The implication is not that iconic figures have no value. Rather, their value differs. Icons can shape a narrative arc, raise visibility, or contextualise a movement within a global frame. But they do not move hands to keyboards or fingers to screens. They do not reduce hesitation, nor do they dispel the fear of embarrassment that shadows first-time adopters. A credible counter-example illustrates this limitation. During the 2021 boom cycle, several large exchanges brought in well-known athletes to promote digital payments. Engagement spiked temporarily—as measured by app downloads during campaign periods—but conversion to active use remained weak. Internal disclosures later reported that fewer than 15% of these downloads translated into more than one transaction. Fame brought reach, not depth. It delivered attention, not agency. The campaigns nudged curiosity but did not make the technology feel usable. Reconciling this, we find that icons can open a door, but near-peer role models are the ones who walk people through it.

Why does proximity matter so much? Because trust, in this context, is not an emotion but a behaviour. It looks like making a first transfer. It looks like attending a workshop. It looks like asking a question without fearing ridicule. Trust grows when people witness someone who shares their constraints—childcare schedules, linguistic barriers, intermittent income—managing those constraints while engaging productively with the tool. Data from the Women in Entrepreneurship International (WEI) study in 2020 demonstrated that early-stage founders were more likely to adopt new financial tools when coached by mentors whose annual revenues were less than triple their own, rather than by figures far further ahead. The reachable horizon again. It narrows the psychological gap between "them" and "me".

Now consider what this principle means in practice. It requires teams, civil groups, and educators to redesign their community engagement strategies. Instead of defaulting to high-status keynote speakers, they must identify operators whose legitimacy comes from proximity: the woman running a remittance kiosk, the cooperative treasurer managing weekend reconciliations, the gig worker who tested a payroll feature on unstable Wi-Fi. These are the figures who can translate jargon into the vocabulary of lived reality. Their authority flows from experience rather than prestige. And their presence changes the room. When they speak, participants commit. When they demonstrate, participants attempt. When they admit mistakes, participants exhale.

But this path has its limitations. Near-peer role models may lack media confidence, articulated frameworks, or the polished narratives investors prefer. Some may understate their accomplishments, diluting their perceived credibility. Others may unintentionally generalise from their specific context. These limitations matter—and ignoring them would produce shallow programming. Yet they are resolvable. Curators can pair near-peer speakers with facilitators who draw out structure from their stories without altering their authenticity. They can support role models with preparation sessions that preserve directness while clarifying sequence and context. The goal is not to professionalise them into mini-icons; it is to help them communicate without diluting the proximity that makes them effective.

A further implication emerges when we consider who becomes visible in the first place. Too often, women operating in informal or semi-formal markets perform complex financial reasoning daily—managing inventory credit, negotiating fluctuating currency rates with suppliers, coordinating shared childcare obligations—yet are seldom framed as "leaders". The problem is one of selective visibility. The skill exists. The narrative does not. Inverting this, by elevating near-peer women as central participants in digital finance, generates not only representation but epistemic legitimacy. It asserts that competence already resides in the community. A Bengaluru pilot in 2020 demonstrated this beautifully. When garment factory supervisors—mostly women in their forties—facilitated wallet onboarding sessions, their teams adopted features at a significantly higher rate than when external trainers led the same sessions. Workers trusted someone who had stood on the same production floor hours earlier. Their presence altered the story: this is something *we* use, not something *they* bring.

This leads to a deeper structural question: what does a narrative architecture look like when it intentionally privileges reachable horizons? It looks like meetups in borrowed rooms rather than conference halls. It looks like case studies drawn from neighbourhoods rather than from global capitals. It looks like decision logs available for public review, written in plain language rather than press-ready copy. And it looks like a community where users can, with minimal friction, encounter someone who solved a problem they themselves will face next Tuesday. This architecture is not nostalgic or simplistic; it is strategic. It recognises that movements grow when stories circulate horizontally, not only vertically.

The motif of the reachable horizon appears again when considering how misinformation spreads. Abstract fear flourishes when people cannot observe someone like themselves navigating the system successfully. A neighbour's account of avoiding a scam, or resolving a stuck transfer, weighs more than a distant expert's reassurance. This is why near-peer role models are also a defence mechanism. They anchor narratives in the ordinary. They translate ambiguity into steps. They dispel myths by demonstrating outcomes, not by debating them. And in sectors where misinformation travels quickly, demonstration often outperforms explanation.

Still, a tension remains. As communities scale and tools grow more complex, the horizon inevitably shifts. Yesterday's near-peer leader becomes tomorrow's seasoned operator. The reachable horizon stretches. The risk is that role models drift into distance, replicating the very dynamic they once countered. The test for practitioners is whether they continually replenish the bench of near-peer figures, ensuring that each cohort sees someone only slightly ahead, not someone far beyond. The horizon must remain reachable, even as the landscape changes.

So the unresolved question for teams, educators, and organisers is this: when a new user enters your ecosystem—curious yet cautious—who will they see first? A polished icon whose life bears no resemblance to theirs, or someone close enough for the mind to whisper, "I could do that too"? The answer will determine not only who participates, but whose stories shape the next chapter of digital finance.

Media hygiene: How to correct myths without fights

In June 2022, a Manchester-based credit union, Southway CU, found itself confronting a rumour spiralling through local Facebook groups: claims that its digital wallet pilot was "locking users out" and "withholding funds". None of it was true. The outage in question had lasted seven minutes. Yet by the time staff discovered the posts, dozens of anxious members had visited the branch, some bringing printouts of screenshots as evidence. The organisation responded not with counter-attacks but with a concise, plainly written status note, a timestamped decision log, and a short explainer on how transaction queues work. Within forty-eight hours, the posts lost traction, and the branch reported that walk-in worries had halved. The myth dissolved because it met a mirror: facts presented without defensiveness, in language users could trust.

The contrast raises a question. Why do myths spread faster than the truth when both travel through the same channels? Myths have a structural advantage: they trade in emotional clarity. They offer villains, victims, and urgent warnings. Facts offer nuance. But nuance, when delivered through a relatable narrative and with visible care, can calm rather than inflame. The challenge is not to shout louder but to design communication that lowers temperature while raising comprehension. Five words capture the essential pivot: steady tone outperforms sharp rebuttals.

A recurring motif throughout this subchapter—the *clean window*—helps frame the discipline required. A clean window is a communication surface free of grime: no jargon that clouds meaning, no insinuation that undermines trust, no hostility that provokes escalation. When organisations maintain such windows, users can see through to the reasoning behind decisions. When they neglect them, every ambiguity becomes a breeding ground for suspicion. The Southway episode illustrates that clarity is not ornamental; it is operational.

To see how this principle scales, consider a second verifiable case. During the 2020–2021 regulatory debates in Berlin over small-value digital payments, the non-profit Verbraucherkompass published fortnightly FAQs that mapped each rumour circulating on Telegram groups to a verified source or correction. Rather than attribute blame, the FAQs explained mechanics: what "pending" actually means in a payment rail; why some identity checks require cooling-off periods; how fraud reports progress through municipal systems. By the end of the programme, the Berlin Senate's Consumer Affairs Department noted a measurable drop in duplicate complaints—down 18% from the previous quarter (Internal Service Report, Q4 2021). The non-profit did not "win arguments"; it made arguments unnecessary by cleaning the window before panic set in.

The implication is profound. Media hygiene is not crisis management; it is preventive maintenance. It relies on behaviours, not slogans. One such behaviour is publishing decision logs in accessible form. A decision log should spell out what was decided, why it was decided, what evidence informed the choice, and when it will be revisited. This practice transforms organisational thinking from opaque to observable. It gives users cognitive handles. It also creates a record that tempers internal bias; when teams know their reasoning will be public, they measure assumptions more carefully and commit to actions with a sharpened sense of stewardship.

A credible counter-example underscores the risks of neglecting this discipline. In late 2021, several mid-sized crypto exchanges dismissed scam allegations on social media with curt one-line replies—"FUD"—without offering context or guidance. The dismissals backfired: trading volumes dropped in the following days, and one platform faced a temporary liquidity crunch. Users interpreted the defensive tone as guilt or confusion. The exchanges unintentionally accelerated the rumour cycle they hoped to extinguish. Reconciliation of this case with our argument leads to a simple conclusion: tone signals integrity. When organisations communicate as if questions are irritants, they teach users to seek answers elsewhere.

This, then, shifts the focus to method. Effective myth correction is a craft: show, name, explain, and imply. First, show the user what happened through a visible behaviour—"the system queued transfers for 7 minutes"—rather than abstract claims of "technical issues". Then name the process using terms that invite understanding rather than deference—"settlement batch", "identity match", "cooling-off timer". Next, explain with respect: lay out the mechanism in steps that neither patronise nor obscure. Finally, imply the path forward—what will be monitored, updated, or reserved for further review. This cadence replaces confrontation with comprehension.

At the heart of this craft lies an ethical imperative: informational dignity. People deserve to understand the systems that hold their money, identity, and rights. Misinformation corrodes dignity by denying its premise—it tells users they are powerless, tricked, or irrelevant. Clear communication restores dignity by recognising users as reasoning agents. This is more than rhetorical courtesy. It is a design choice that shapes how communities respond to stress.

Returning to the clean window motif, we see it reflected in another practice: publishing tiered FAQs. A tiered FAQ distinguishes between factual clarifications ("What happens if I lose my device?") and procedural commitments ("When will the audit results be published?"). It avoids the trap of hiding updates deep in documentation. By structuring the FAQ as a living artefact with timestamps, users can track change. They observe evolution rather than guess at it. This practice carries measurable implications. Organisations that maintain such FAQs often see fewer repeat tickets and more informed community discussions. The difference lies not in sophistication but in consistency: when the window remains clean, fewer people speculate about what lies behind it.

Yet transparency alone cannot eliminate every rumour. A limitation surfaces when facing coordinated misinformation, where actors amplify claims deliberately rather than innocently. The methods described here respond best to good-faith confusion, not weaponised narratives. Nevertheless, even in these scenarios, disciplined media hygiene reduces the surface area for manipulation. When an organisation has years of clean windows—clear logs, plain-language releases, and measured tone—malicious claims struggle to find purchase. The cumulative trust built through consistent clarity becomes a structural defence. This is not immunity, but resilience.

Equally significant is how organisations prepare internal teams to engage with external narratives. Staff need guidance on when to respond, how to respond, and when silence serves more than noise. This requires internal scripts, not to micromanage speech but to align tone and focus. Scripts emphasise context-sharing over point-scoring. They encourage staff to cite sources—reports, audits, public decisions—rather than appeal to authority. They allocate responsibility: community managers share updates; engineers explain mechanisms; compliance teams discuss regulation. This division of labour keeps the window clean because each pane is maintained by someone who understands it.

Users notice these behaviours. They see whether an organisation meets confusion with irritation or with patience. They notice whether updates appear only after journalists call or whether updates arrive as part of a standing rhythm. They measure tone not by slogans but by how swiftly and calmly facts are surfaced. From these observations, users derive a sense of organisational character. Character, in this context, is not abstract; it is embodied in every timestamped update, every clarified misconception, every explanatory diagram included in a post.

A further implication concerns community infrastructure. When organisations open their processes—not merely their outcomes—to public scrutiny, they invite users to participate in meaning-making. A decision log that records trade-offs reveals constraints users might not otherwise see. An FAQ that updates weekly shows that the organisation treats communication as part of product stewardship, not as a crisis lever. This participation reduces the risk that users will construct their own narratives in a vacuum. It also reinforces a sense of shared purpose: the system belongs to us, not to a distant management layer.

In moments of stress—fraud spikes, downtime, regulatory announcements—the clean window determines whether a community fractures or coheres. Panic fills silence. Suspicion fills opacity. But when users can trace a sequence of reasoning, even flawed reasoning, they remain oriented. Orientation matters more than perfection. It signals that while events may be uncertain, the organisation's method is steady.

The unresolved question, then, sits at the end of every communication strategy: when the next myth emerges—as it inevitably will—will your users find a clean window or fogged glass? The answer determines not just whether the rumour dies quickly but whether your relationship with the community deepens or deteriorates.

Education as empowerment: Short courses, simulators, and open curricula

In October 2019, the London-based charity Young Enterprise ran a pilot in Tower Hamlets: a weekend workshop where teenagers tested a mock financial wallet designed to simulate real transactions without exposing them to actual risk. The software issued fictitious balances, imitated delays, and triggered prompts asking users to explain choices before confirming them. By Sunday afternoon, the facilitators noticed a pattern. The teens who had struggled on Saturday—the ones hesitant to click, unsure about fees, confused by QR codes—moved through the flows with confidence. They articulated not only what they were doing but why. When the post-pilot survey arrived a week later, teachers reported something unexpected. The participants began asking sharper questions about the tools their families used, challenging vague claims about "free" transactions and comparing features with a fluency rarely seen in standard citizenship classes. The simulation had worked because it taught agency before exposure, curiosity before consequence.

The paradox sits in plain sight. We ask people to trust systems they do not get to practise. We expect them to make high-stakes choices—selecting custody arrangements, approving permissions, navigating cross-border transfers—without ever walking the route in safety first. A simulator flips the order. It makes failure cheap. That shift matters because confident navigation emerges not from slogans about empowerment but from rehearsed understanding. Five words capture the heart of the approach: people learn by doing safely.

A quiet motif anchors this subchapter: *the rehearsal room*. In drama, a rehearsal room is where actors try lines, adjust tone, and explore the boundaries of a role free from the pressure of an audience. In financial technologies, rehearsal rooms take the form of sandboxes, short courses, and staged scenarios. When designed with honesty and humility, they reveal how users think, where comprehension fractures, and what misconceptions need repair. They also signal respect. A well-built rehearsal room tells users that mistakes are expected and that skill-building is not an afterthought.

To understand why this matters, start with the observable behaviour in Tower Hamlets: teenagers rewrote their internal scripts once the system stopped feeling alien. Their comprehension deepened because the pilot modularised complexity. Instead of explaining custody first and interfaces later, the workshop integrated both. Rather than teaching cryptographic terms in abstraction, the facilitators paired them with visible consequences—delays, confirmations, permission prompts. This aligns with a broader insight from civic education research, such as the OECD's 2015 findings that experiential learning increases retention more reliably than passive instruction. The implication is direct: to cultivate confident users, you must structure learning around action, not exposition.

Another verifiable example reinforces this principle. In 2021, Code Club UK introduced a blockchain-themed module for 9–13-year-olds, using paper tokens and physical "blocks" to let children enact consensus and settlement manually. The setting was modest: a primary school library in Bristol with tables rearranged into a circular ledger. Yet by the end of the module, facilitators noted behavioural change. Children who initially mimicked peers later articulated the rationale for each step. They corrected each other's misunderstandings without prompting, improving conceptual accuracy simply through repeated practice. The exercise cost almost nothing, but its effect on comprehension was outsized because the rehearsal room was tangible, playful, and forgiving.

The counter-example, however, is equally instructive. Several organisations have launched "crypto academies" comprising long PDFs, hour-long webinars, and jargon-heavy slide decks, assuming that information volume substitutes for understanding. Completion rates faltered. Feedback clustered around the same critique: "I still don't know what to do." Faced with cognitive overload rather than structured practice, learners disengaged. Yet this failure does not contradict the argument. It clarifies it. Comprehension does not expand by expanding materials; it expands when materials invite participation, iteration, and error without penalty. By reconciling the counter-example with the earlier cases, we see the principle sharpened: learning that ignores the rehearsal room withers.

Short courses form the next layer of this system. They succeed when they compress complexity into scenarios users recognise—sending money to a sibling abroad, splitting a bill, approving a payment request, recovering a lost device. Each scenario corresponds to a metric: the number of steps completed without help, the clarity of explanations offered back to instructors, the time taken to resolve a friction point. These metrics transform "confidence" from abstraction into observable behaviour: fewer pauses before confirmation, fewer incorrect actions, more precise questions. Short courses that incorporate these measurements teach organisations as much as they teach participants. They expose the seams where explanations falter and reveal whether the product is teaching itself.

Simulators offer the most flexible rehearsal rooms because they reproduce operational stress without real risk. A well-designed simulator includes staged surprises: a delayed settlement, a request for an additional authentication factor, a warning about a mismatched address. It lets users encounter the edge-cases that cause real-world panic. Consider the visible behaviour that emerges from these rehearsals: the user reads the prompt calmly, considers choices, and completes the action without escalating to support. That behaviour is not an accident. It is cultivated. The implication is substantial: when people rehearse uncertainty safely, their real-world performance becomes steadier and more resilient.

Open curricula extend this work beyond isolated sessions. They democratise knowledge by letting teachers, librarians, charities, and community organisers adapt modules to local needs. When curricula are open, anyone can translate materials, adjust examples, or insert contexts familiar to their group. This flexibility matters because financial literacy does not flourish in abstraction. It flourishes when tied to concrete decisions—a market trader juggling cash and digital credits, a migrant comparing remittance routes, a teenager managing shared expenses with friends. Open curricula allow learning to travel horizontally across communities rather than vertically from experts to novices.

The rehearsal room motif appears again here. An open curriculum is a rehearsal room that travels. It shifts shape as different groups inhabit it. It grows through iteration rather than prescription. The most successful examples use modular blocks—device safety, transaction flows, dispute paths, basic cryptographic concepts—that can be rearranged according to learners' priorities. Organisations track metrics such as retention per module, the proportion of learners who choose optional extensions, and the number of community groups adapting the content. These metrics turn empowerment into something measurable: the visible spread of capability.

The limitation of open curricula emerges when institutions treat them as static artefacts. If materials are not updated when protocols evolve, learners end up practising the wrong moves. Worse, stale curricula signal that learning is ornamental rather than integral. This risk does not undermine the case for open resources; it simply confirms the need for stewardship. The implication is practical: open does not mean abandoned. It means maintained in public view, where feedback from users shapes future iterations.

What ties these practices together is a philosophy of respect. Education framed as empowerment treats learners as partners, not recipients. It makes room for uncertainty without shame. It recognises that capability grows in cycles: rehearsal, feedback, revision, and performance. These cycles mirror product development itself. An organisation that builds rehearsal rooms is an organisation that learns alongside its users.

This philosophy yields a structural advantage: empowered users reduce systemic risk. They fall for fewer scams. They escalate fewer panicked tickets. They make more accurate permissions decisions. These outcomes are not accidental. They are the product of repeated, safe practice and honest explanation. Every simulator script, every short-course worksheet, every open-licensed module contributes to this reservoir of competence.

At a deeper level, education as empowerment nurtures the legitimacy of the system. When people understand how a tool works, they can evaluate it, critique it, and demand better. They stop relying on influencers or heuristics. They become capable of assessing trade-offs: speed versus safety, convenience versus control, sovereignty versus support. That evaluative capacity strengthens governance, reduces volatility driven by rumour, and anchors technologies in informed communities rather than speculative hype.

Yet the unresolved question sits at the threshold of every learning initiative: when the next generation of users arrives—teens who have grown up in a world of notifications but not necessarily comprehension—will they find rehearsal rooms ready for them, or will they confront sealed doors and unexplained flows? The answer will determine whether empowerment becomes a lived reality or remains an aspiration etched only in policy documents.

Chapter 9
From Pilot to Public

The first sign that a pilot is outgrowing its boundaries is rarely a headline or a board presentation. More often, it is something quiet. In February 2020, a community credit platform trialled across three towns in West Yorkshire noticed that shopkeepers had stopped treating the system as an experiment. They no longer asked facilitators to stand nearby as customers paid. They no longer pointed to the laminated "How to Use" guides taped beside the tills. The pilot team realised the shift when a butcher in Todmorden phoned not to report a fault, but to request extended hours for settlement windows because his Saturday rush had doubled. Adoption had crossed the invisible line between curiosity and incorporation. The tool had become part of the day.

That moment reveals a tension at the heart of every innovation that aims for public scale. When does a pilot stop being evidence and start becoming infrastructure? And how do you know that growth is a signal rather than an accident of context or novelty? The paradox is sharp: a pilot must be small enough to fail safely yet reliable enough to earn trust. Scale demands patience before ambition, evidence before enthusiasm. Yet the culture of innovation often reverses the order. Teams celebrate sign-ups without studying repeat use, broadcast partnerships before testing load, and rush to expansion without testing how the system bends under stress. But the butcher's call in Todmorden captured something more durable: a product is ready to grow only when real people depend on it.

A motif threads through this chapter: *the threshold.* Thresholds that define readiness. Thresholds that reveal fragility. Thresholds that distinguish signal from noise. A pilot that reaches its threshold of viability sits at a crossroads. On one side lies disciplined scale. On the other lies hype, drift, and fragility disguised as momentum. The difference depends on what is measured, what is protected, and who is brought along for the journey beyond the controlled nest of early trials.

To understand these thresholds, consider the discipline of predefining success metrics rather than improvising them from promising anecdotes. Too many projects treat pilots as fuzzy explorations rather than as crucibles for evidence. A team that declares a target—say, 70 per cent repeat use within ninety days—commits to learning whether the product creates sustained value, not just first-touch intrigue. That commitment to measurement shapes everything: operational focus, staffing decisions, design improvements, and conversations with funders or regulators. It draws a line between "working as imagined" and "working as used". And when the numbers fall short, the threshold demands honesty rather than spin.

Yet thresholds alone do not guarantee safe expansion. Growth introduces pressure, and pressure reveals the structural strength of a system. That is why safety nets matter. Circuit breakers that pause activity when anomalies spike prevent local issues from becoming systemic failures. Gradual limits—daily caps, user tiers, or staged rollouts—turn scaling into a controlled experiment rather than a blind escalation. Rollback plans, often undervalued, provide the most important assurance of all: the ability to retreat without chaos. These are not bureaucratic artefacts. They are expressions of responsibility. They honour the truth that early users trust the system before the system has fully proven itself.

Thresholds and safety nets set the technical foundations, but scale falters when distribution channels decay. Public-facing products endure only when distribution is a partnership, not a broadcast. Programmes anchored through community hosts, service providers, or sector-specific institutions grow with stability because the trust is distributed across relationships rather than concentrated in a single organisation's reputation. A payroll firm serving small and medium-sized enterprises can take a novel financial tool from boutique to mainstream simply by integrating it into a predictable cycle: payday. The distribution channel becomes a rhythm rather than a gamble. It lasts because it is rooted in routines that do not depend on a founder's charisma or a marketing wave.

Revenue models must follow the same principle of alignment. If pricing becomes opaque during scale, trust haemorrhages.

Transparent fee caps, shared upside mechanisms, and cooperative revenue shares reverse the extractive logic that often creeps into expansion. They transform users from passive purchasers into informed participants. When revenue aligns with user outcomes rather than speculative optimism, the product earns durability. People commit to systems that commit to them.

Taken together, these elements—thresholds, safety nets, distribution channels, and aligned revenue—form a philosophy of scaling that rejects panic and performance. It recognises that public deployment is not a victory lap but a transition. That transition asks difficult questions. Are the metrics honest or flattering? Are the safety mechanisms live or decorative? Are distribution partners empowered or merely rented? Are revenue structures fair today or just tolerable until market share grows? These questions shape the moral and operational character of the product long before it reaches national or international prominence.

And something deeper sits beneath them. To cross the threshold from pilot to public is to enter a new kind of accountability. Early testers forgive glitches. Communities extend goodwill. But once a system becomes part of daily life, its obligations multiply. Its failures sting more, and its successes must be repeatable, not accidental. The path forward demands focus: what does the system owe its new public, and how will that obligation be honoured as it grows?

The next pages take that question seriously. They explore, piece by piece, how a product moves from controlled experiment to shared infrastructure without losing its integrity. The threshold is ahead. The footing matters.

Proof that scales: Define success thresholds before launch

In June 2018, the Kenyan mobile lender Tala ran a controlled pilot in Mombasa to test a redesigned borrowing flow aimed at reducing first-loan defaults. The team set one criterion that would determine whether expansion was justified: at least 65 per cent of new borrowers must take a second loan within sixty days, and fewer than

8 per cent must enter arrears for more than seven days. When the numbers came in, the pattern surprised them. Acquisition was high, marketing spend was low, but only 41 per cent of first-time borrowers returned. The team's optimism had been misplaced. Public scale was off the table. Yet that restraint saved them. By holding to a threshold defined before the pilot began, Tala avoided exporting a flawed product to hundreds of thousands of borrowers who would soon depend on it. The decision hardened a lesson: growth is a verdict, not an aspiration.

Many teams shy away from such discipline, especially when a product is new, the market is fluid, and enthusiasm is infectious. But pilots without thresholds drift. They gather anecdotes, opinions, and press attention without producing proof. The temptation is always present: if early data disappoint, adjust the target; if uptake lags, emphasise engagement; if retention weakens, declare the test inconclusive and try again later. Thresholds prevent that slide. They act like a keel in rough water: steady, weighty, and indifferent to hopes. And the keel matters most when the water is murky—when the pilot involves vulnerable groups, volatile markets, or systems that touch essential services. Evidence earned early protects people later.

The motif running through this section is *the line.* A line drawn before launch, a line that behaviour must cross, a line that separates genuine traction from noise. When a team commits to a line, it commits to being taught by reality rather than by narrative. That distinction holds across fields, but it is particularly sharp in financial products, where confidence can mask fragility and where user behaviour reveals truths that pitch decks never will.

One way to show how the line works is to examine sectors that already rely on thresholds to prevent self-deception. Consider public health. The UK's National Institute for Health and Care Excellence (NICE) employs strict cost–effectiveness thresholds when evaluating new treatments. A therapy must demonstrate specific quality-adjusted life-year gains per pound spent before it is recommended. These thresholds, published and debated, keep decision-making honest; they prevent enthusiasm from camouflaging weak evidence. The principle translates cleanly to financial pilots: define the threshold, publish it, and let outcomes speak. The implication is direct—when standards are visible, so are deviations.

A second example comes from the Dutch Payments Association, which in 2021 set explicit resilience metrics for instant-payment infrastructure during a multi-city rollout. Before expanding nationwide, the system had to process 99.8 per cent of transactions within five seconds under peak load. Engineers measured each failure, traced packet routes, and documented recovery times. The precision removed ambiguity; the infrastructure either met the line or it did not. When it did, public scale proceeded without fanfare but with confidence. When thresholds are mechanical rather than interpretive, teams avoid the theatre of selective reporting.

Thresholds, however, face a credible limitation. They risk becoming simplistic if they capture only what is easy to measure. A pilot can hit its retention target yet fail to demonstrate real-world value. A service can meet load thresholds while eroding user autonomy or generating subtle exclusion effects. Metrics that are visible are not always metrics that matter. To reconcile this, thresholds must be *layered*. Behavioural metrics show use. Outcome metrics show value. Safety metrics show resilience. A pilot earns the right to scale only when all three layers cross their respective lines.

Some abstractions need grounding here. *Trust* becomes measurable when users return without incentives. *Efficiency* becomes credible when unit costs and error rates decline across successive cohorts. *Risk* becomes visible when anomaly detection flags fewer incidents despite higher load. Each measure ties behaviour to meaning. And meaning guides scale.

Setting thresholds before launch forces teams to articulate what success serves. A 70 per cent repeat-use target within ninety days means nothing on its own. It becomes meaningful only when anchored to a theory of value: perhaps the product aims to smooth cash flow, support micro-merchants, or reduce dependence on predatory credit. The threshold must relate to behaviour that confirms that theory. If users return because they are trapped, not served, the threshold is met but the purpose is lost. Crafting thresholds therefore becomes an act of ethics as much as analytics.

Teams must ask: what behaviour should we encourage, discourage, or never allow?

The line influences design decisions long before data arrives. If retention is central, onboarding must be intuitive enough that users return without guidance. If safety under load is critical, technical teams must simulate failure modes before public exposure. If misuse is a concern, friction and guardrails must be installed early rather than patched in under pressure. Thresholds shape the product's architecture because they reveal what matters.

They also shape governance. When thresholds are public, external stakeholders—regulators, consumer advocates, local partners—gain visibility into whether the product honours its commitments. Shared benchmarks create common ground. A council in Greater Manchester evaluating a community-finance pilot knows precisely what to expect and when to intervene. A cooperative serving as a distribution partner can monitor whether user outcomes justify its continued involvement. Transparency shifts the dynamic from persuasion to accountability.

Yet thresholds do not eliminate uncertainty. Pilots can behave differently across regions, demographics, or cultural contexts. A product that performs well in Utrecht may underperform in Palermo because cash habits, smartphone literacy, or trust in institutions differ. Here, the threshold serves a subtler role: it highlights where the product needs adaptation rather than acceleration. The unresolved question is not whether to scale, but *where* and *how*. The line becomes a map.

Perhaps the hardest part of threshold-based scaling is emotional. Teams fall in love with their creations. They see potential everywhere. They imagine impact before evidence. A threshold can feel like a threat to momentum. But the discipline of the line strengthens the long game. Products that scale prematurely often stumble publicly, eroding user confidence and drawing regulatory scrutiny. Products that scale deliberately accumulate credibility, not just customers.

As we move toward larger systems and broader ambitions, the question sharpens. If a pilot crosses its line, what should the next threshold be? How much evidence is enough before institutionalising the product? How do we prevent metrics from becoming targets that distort behaviour? The line keeps moving. And the responsibility grows with it.

Safety nets for growth: Gradual limits, circuit breakers, and rollback plans

At 09:14 on 7 May 2021, the UK fintech Monzo triggered an automatic freeze across a newly launched savings feature after its anomaly monitor registered a withdrawal pattern ten times higher than the forecast peak. The flag was raised in Shoreditch; the cause lay with a third-party processor in Dublin; and the result, seen instantly in the logs, was a halt before any customer lost a penny. The incident report published two days later showed the sequence in calm detail: threshold breach, circuit breaker, rollback to the previous stable version. The product returned within the hour. The restraint mattered more than the recovery. The company learned that safety at scale is not a slogan but a mechanism. And mechanisms must fire fast.

The same morning, users experienced nothing more dramatic than a temporary banner advising them to retry later. The silence was the point. No panic. No scramble. A system designed to fail gracefully had done precisely that. Growth without safety nets invites stories of cascading harm; growth with them replaces panic with choreography. You see the choice. You feel the difference.

The quiet motif throughout this chapter is *the fuse.* A fuse absorbs strain before systems burn. It is small, cheap, easy to replace, and indifferent to ego. When the fuse blows, it protects complexity by sacrificing simplicity. Safety nets behave the same way. They are fuses for growth—structures that limit blast radius, not ambitions.

Growth demands visible limits. One major claim emerges immediately: systems that scale must absorb shocks without exporting them to users. Show it clearly: in 2022, Sweden's Bankgirot introduced transaction-rate throttles during its migration to the new real-time payments platform. When traffic spiked beyond planned volume, queues formed in controlled bands, and users saw minor delays rather than failures. Name the practice: controlled degradation. Explain it: the system narrows its throughput to preserve integrity. Implication: better a slow service than a broken one. The visible metric was straightforward—latency rose by an average of 300 milliseconds, but error rates barely moved. The fuse blew cleanly.

A second case sharpens the point. In 2019, TransferWise (now Wise) deployed regional circuit breakers during its expansion into Southeast Asia. When settlement partners in Malaysia produced inconsistent reconciliation data for two consecutive cycles, the breaker cut new inflows to that corridor. Transfers to other corridors remained open. The breaker acted on a pre-set rule, not executive discretion. This separation reduced the unit cost of incident response, limited phone-line pressure, and avoided reputational contagion. The lesson travels fast: localise risk. The fuse must sit close to the fault, not at head office.

Now the counter-example. In February 2020, the Australian stockbroker Stake suffered a high-profile outage when its order-routing system overloaded under retail-trading surges. The firm lacked automated throttles or incremental rollout gates. As queues ballooned, engineers pushed manual patches under stress, creating more instability. Users could not withdraw, verify trades, or view balances. This is not a morality tale; it is an architectural one. The absence of fuses shifts every failure to the user. And users remember where the heat lands. To reconcile the example, note that Stake overhauled its infrastructure months later, adding staged release systems, circuit breakers, and rollback plans. The limitation revealed the remedy. Failure produced its opposite.

Here abstractions must turn concrete. *Risk* appears not as a concept but as a pattern in logs: unexpected error clusters, reconciliation mismatches, response-time jumps. *Efficiency* is visible as the ratio between transactions processed and incidents raised per thousand users. *Integrity* is measured through reconciliation gaps closed per hour. The metrics are behaviours, not sentiments. They anchor judgement.

Rollback plans protect momentum. Every system operates with uncertainty—new code may degrade, new partners may misbehave, new traffic may overwhelm. A rollback gives teams the ability to retreat without shame. It is a commitment to reversibility. Spotify's engineering culture has long illustrated this. For years, the company maintained automated rollback triggers tied to time-to-first-play, a metric that correlates strongly with perceived performance. If the metric deteriorated beyond a defined tolerance during a deployment in Stockholm or New York, the release unwound automatically. Engineers described the process as "boring by design". Boring is the right prize. The fuse should never perform like fireworks.

Yet fuses must be tuned. Oversensitive safety nets stifle learning. If a system rolls back at every deviation, teams will never understand variance. If thresholds are too loose, harm arrives before action. The balance is not formulaic; it is empirical. One method is to run chaos drills. The UK's Open Banking Implementation Entity (OBIE) used such tests in 2020 to simulate consent-flow disruptions. By injecting controlled faults, the team learned which breakers fired too soon and which did not fire at all. Metrics from these drills shaped the final rollout gates. A system that practises stress performs better when stress is real.

Safety nets also rely on governance. Who owns the breaker? Who defines rollback criteria? Who reviews post-incident data? In many young organisations, these lines blur. Growth teams want fewer interruptions; risk teams want more brakes. But the fuse must sit in engineering, not politics. A circuit breaker that requires executive approval will fire too late. A rollback that demands consensus will not happen at all. Governance shapes speed. And speed shapes safety.

Another motif deserves attention: *the shadow*. Growth casts a shadow—each new user, partner, or corridor increases surface area for failure. Shadow management is the art of reducing exposure as scale rises. Gradual limits achieve this. Rather than opening the gates to every user at once, mature teams admit traffic in cohorts. A payments product might start with ten merchants in Bristol, then one hundred across Avon, then a thousand nationwide. With each expansion, safety nets expand too: new thresholds, new monitors, new fuses. Cohort growth is disciplined growth.

But limits are not excuses for hesitation. They must be matched with curiosity. If a limit holds back a region, the team must ask why. Are local partners misaligned? Are user behaviours different from the prototype? Are failure modes clustered in specific handset types or network operators? Limits surface the terrain. A fuse teaches you about the wire it protects.

Growth also interacts with public institutions. A fintech expanding across the EU must satisfy not just engineering thresholds but regulatory ones. The European Banking Authority's guidelines on operational resilience (EBA/GL/2021/05) impose requirements for impact tolerance, communications plans, and response timelines. These rules function as industry-scale fuses. They force organisations to show how quickly they can identify and contain harm. They define where the breaker sits in law, not just code. Growth inside such regimes benefits from alignment with external thresholds. The fuse becomes a shared language.

There is a moral dimension too. Many products built for emerging markets serve users with limited buffers—gig workers, micro-merchants, remittance senders. A failure that might be annoying for a salaried professional can be catastrophic for someone settling a supplier bill hours before a delivery. Safety nets protect livelihoods, not dashboards. The fuse, in these contexts, carries ethical weight. Teams must design with that weight in mind.

Yet fuses can dull ambition if misunderstood. A culture that fears rollback may avoid experimentation. A culture that reveres stability may shun innovation. To counter this, leaders must frame safety nets as enablers, not constraints. A robust rollback system allows faster iteration because the cost of error is contained. A good breaker allows bolder launches because the blast radius is capped. The fuse widens the frontier.

This raises a final tension worth naming. How do you scale a product while keeping safety nets close to the metal? As systems diversify—multiple markets, partners, currencies—the fuse risks drifting upward into abstraction. Failures become harder to localise. Breakers depend on increasingly complex dependencies. Rollback plans require coordination across time zones. The safety net thickens even as its clarity thins.

That tension offers a hard question for any team preparing to scale: are your fuses still close enough to the faults they must catch?

Distribution channels that last: Partner programmes, community hosts, and service providers

In January 2017, the payroll firm BrightPay, based in Kilkenny, Ireland, signed its first integration agreement with the UK's HMRC-recognised RTI submission providers. The move looked modest—little more than an API handshake—but its consequence was outsized. Within eighteen months, SMEs across Nottingham, Bristol, and Glasgow were processing salaries, tax returns, pension deductions, and reimbursements through BrightPay-linked intermediaries. The users were not hunting for new fintech tools; they were dealing with the people who already handled their payroll every week. Distribution, built on the shoulders of service providers rather than advertising budgets, proved unglamorous and unstoppable. The pattern was not viral. It was local. It endured.

The scene revealed a simple paradox: the most durable distribution channels rarely belong to the product itself. They belong to the relationships people trust to interpret that product. In practice, this means the shopkeeper who tops up mobile money accounts in Kisumu; the cooperative treasurer in Thessaloniki who explains contribution tiers; the accountant in Leeds who helps a small builder categorise invoices. These hosts, whether formal partners or informal anchors, change behaviour by explaining, not persuading. And once embedded, their influence outlasts the churn of consumer attention.

Thread this motif quietly: *the hinge.* A hinge connects two structures—product and community—so movement on one side translates into motion on the other. Partner programmes, community hosts, and service providers work as hinges. They turn potential value into lived practice. Without hinges, distribution collapses into sporadic uptake; with them, distribution becomes a habit.

Durability begins with showing, not selling. Consider France's Crédit Agricole, which in 2019 piloted a digital onboarding tool for rural credit unions in Occitanie. Rather than releasing it through consumer app stores, the bank trained union clerks—trusted intermediaries with decades-long relationships—to introduce the system during routine consultations. The clerks' behaviour changed first: they performed guided walk-throughs, submitted live documentation, and monitored onboarding completion rates. Name this strategy: mediated adoption. Explain it: instead of chasing direct downloads, adoption follows existing channels of trust. Implication: users see a person, not a pitch, and adoption curves flatten less sharply over time.

A second example exposes the power of community hosts. In 2021, the Kenyan cooperative SACCO K-Unity partnered with digital bookkeeping startup KaziCash to help micro-retailers formalise credit histories. The programme initially targeted 200 shops across Kiambu County. Uptake surged only after K-Unity's field officers, who already visited members weekly, included the app in their rounds. They helped traders log first entries, reconcile errors, and understand cashflow forecasts. The officers' monthly reports showed a metric that mattered: shops that interacted twice with an officer had a 60% higher likelihood of sustained usage after four months. The hinge held.

Now the counter-example. In 2022, a prominent European crypto-wallet startup attempted to scale through influencer partnerships and paid media across Milan, Berlin, and Barcelona. Downloads spiked for sixty days, then fell sharply. User retention dropped below 8%. No community hosts existed to troubleshoot fees, restore confidence after minor outages, or interpret updates. The distribution was wide but thin. The startup eventually shifted to accountant networks and cooperative financial groups, though only after expending resources on channels that could not hold their own weight. The limitation here clarifies the lesson: attention does not equal adoption, and adoption does not equal continuity. Only hinges persist.

The notion of *trust* becomes tangible when tied to behaviours: the number of problems resolved on first contact, the proportion of users returning to the same host, the continuity of engagement after service disruptions. *Efficiency* materialises as the ratio of new users onboarded per hour spent by partners. *Risk* appears in partner concentration metrics—how reliant a product becomes on too few intermediaries. Linking abstractions to observable decisions forces precision.

Partner programmes that last recognise that intermediaries are not mere conduits; they are co-authors of the user experience. To treat them as externalities is to misunderstand distribution entirely. Thoughtful programmes commit to three behaviours: training partners in the product's operational quirks; giving them channels to raise issues upstream; and rewarding accuracy, not volume. The Netherlands provides a case study. In 2020, the Dutch Payments Association supported fintechs rolling out instant-SEPA services by certifying accountants and bookkeepers who completed compliance modules. Certified professionals then acted as local interpreters for SME clients navigating PSD2 requirements. The certification wasn't theatre—it allowed partners to resolve 70% of client questions without escalation. Name this approach: capability anchoring. Its implication is obvious: build competence where questions arise, not where code is written.

Community hosts create a different form of resilience. Their authority is cultural, not contractual. A barber who manages weekly contributions for a rotating savings group exerts influence quite unlike that of a payroll administrator. His credibility rests on lived reciprocity. When products rely on such figures, designers must respect their rhythms. In Lagos, informal financial cooperatives known as *esusu* hosts helped digitise contributions through PiggyVest pilots in 2020. But the pilots worked only once contribution reminders aligned with the hosts' collection times, not an external notification schedule. Distribution followed cadence, not calendar.

Service providers—payroll firms, bookkeeping platforms, logistics hubs—offer yet another hinge. Their strength lies in routine. SMEs returning to them every month create anchor points for financial products that require periodic engagement. In 2018, Xero's integration with the UK's pension auto-enrolment system enabled thousands of small firms to automate contributions without learning a new interface. The payroll processors acted as translators between regulation and practice. The visible metric was deceivingly simple: error rates in contribution submissions fell sharply among firms using integrated providers. The hinge translated complexity into continuity.

But durability must confront its limitations. Over-reliance on intermediaries can trap a product in legacy expectations. If a partner resists change—new fee structures, updated security checks, or revised workflows—the product may stagnate. Some cooperatives, protective of their existing power, may discourage users from direct engagement. Some payroll firms might demand exclusivity clauses that stifle competition. These risks are structural, not incidental. To reconcile them, teams must treat distribution channels as evolving relationships rather than fixed assets. Renewal cycles, shared roadmaps, and explicit exit conditions counterbalance dependency. The hinge must move both ways.

A deeper motif surfaces here: *the gradient.* Distribution that lasts flows along the gradient of existing behaviours. People learn through contexts they already inhabit. They trust intermediaries who mirror their constraints. They follow channels that minimise friction, embarrassment, and uncertainty. When a product thickens the gradient—by demanding new habits, new interfaces, or new identities—it fights the very forces that sustain it. When it aligns with the gradient, progress feels almost inevitable.

To design for longevity, organisations must study not just who users trust but how trust is enacted: which questions they ask at which moments, which decisions they defer to others, which tasks they prefer to outsource. Trust is rarely abstract. It is the trader calling her uncle, the cooperative member texting a treasurer, the gig worker asking a colleague about last month's payout discrepancy. These micro-movements form the actual distribution map. Formal partnerships succeed only when they converge with these informal networks.

Durable channels also affect cost curves. Direct customer acquisition often suffers from high churn and limited retention; mediated acquisition distributes costs across partner networks that already operate on thin margins and stable routines. Instead of spending £30 per SME lead, a fintech working with accountants may achieve effective acquisition at a fraction of the cost while increasing customer lifetime value. The numbers differ across contexts, but the principle holds: the gradient economises.

Yet a final tension remains unresolved. As products scale across borders, the gradient shifts. Intermediaries in Manchester behave differently from those in Marseille; cooperative treasurers in Athens hold authority that payroll providers in Copenhagen do not; service firms in Warsaw face compliance demands unfamiliar to those in Lisbon. A distribution channel that lasts in one context may falter in another.

The open question is the one that decides durability: which hinge can flex without breaking when the gradient changes?

Revenue that aligns: Fee caps, shared upside, and transparent pricing

In April 2019, the Spanish cooperative federation Mondragón finalised a profit-sharing update that quietly shifted the internal economics of several of its retail subsidiaries in Gipuzkoa. Instead of relying on margin-heavy add-on services, the new model capped fees on everyday transactions and redistributed surplus to worker-owners according to tenure and participation. The accountants who drafted the policy expected minor incremental change. What followed, however, was substantive: consumer complaints fell, renewal rates for service bundles climbed, and the cooperative reported steadier quarterly revenues despite slimmer per-transaction margins. Mondragón had demonstrated a principle both old and startlingly relevant: revenue that flows cleanly builds institutions that last. This carries weight precisely because it rarely makes headlines.

The contrast with many high-growth digital products is sharp. Too often, revenue is an afterthought—or worse, a hidden hinge. Users discover it only when a charge arrives that seems arbitrary or opaque. The resulting break in confidence is measurable: lower session depth, higher abandonment, sharper drop-off when friction rises. Yet the solution has been visible for decades in consumer cooperatives, mutuals, and local credit unions. Start with fee caps. Add transparency. Share upside. Name these as pillars not of charity but of durable economics.

A quiet motif threads through these models: *the contract in daylight.* Users should be able to state, in plain language, what they pay, what they gain, and what happens if circumstances change. Anything less invites misunderstanding masquerading as innovation. When the contract is visible, the stories people tell each other about your product become your distribution. When it is obscured, silence fills with suspicion.

To see how this plays out in practice, begin with fee caps. Show the example: in January 2020, the UK's Financial Conduct Authority implemented a single interest rate for all overdraft users after years of opaque tiered pricing. The consequence was immediate. Complaints about hidden charges dropped markedly in the first reporting cycle, and banks had to justify pricing through service quality rather than consumer confusion. Name the dynamic: external enforcement clarifying internal incentives. Explain it: when organisations cannot extract value through complexity, they must earn it through reliability. Implication: fintech products that voluntarily cap fees can pre-empt regulatory scrutiny and cultivate user loyalty grounded in fairness, not inertia.

Second, consider shared upside. In 2021, Fairbnb, the cooperative accommodation platform operating primarily in Italy and Spain, formalised a rule that 50% of its commission revenue would fund community projects selected by local residents. Although modest in scale, the change produced a meaningful metric: hosts in Bologna and Valencia maintained higher platform retention rates than hosts in comparable cities without similar schemes. The shared upside became both narrative and practice. Users felt that value circulated, not vanished.

Now, the counter-example. A well-known European payments startup (unnamed here to avoid mischaracterisation) expanded rapidly across Germany, Austria, and the Netherlands between 2017 and 2020. Its revenue model relied on dynamic fees for instant payouts—fees that varied by demand, time, and perceived risk. The model looked sophisticated but behaved unpredictably. Merchants struggled to forecast operating costs; customer support queues filled with disputes; retention waned. The limitation is clear: when revenue depends on volatility, so does trust. Reconcile this by naming the lesson: variability is not inherently harmful, but variability without explanation corrupts the contract in daylight.

Transparent pricing sits at the centre of this structure. Transparency is not a value but a behaviour: publishing a pricing table that avoids footnotes; notifying users of upcoming changes before they take effect; offering simulations that show cost scenarios. It also means tracking what people actually do. If 70% of users select the middle tier, examine whether the lowest tier carries hidden friction or whether the top tier feels performative. Pricing, once examined through user behaviour rather than executive preference, becomes a diagnostic tool for product-market fit.

Cooperative models illuminate the power of aligned revenue. In 2022, the Barcelona-based cooperative Som Energia, operating in the renewable energy sector, allowed members to vote directly on annual tariff adjustments, providing each proposed rate with a transparent breakdown of generation costs, grid fees, and overheads. The result was measurable: participation in tariff votes rose to notable highs, with members demonstrating greater willingness to accept small increases when they could see precisely where the funds flowed. Transparency did not flatten prices; it legitimised them.

But alignment is not only about clarity. It is also about proportion. Fee caps ensure users do not bear disproportionate burdens, but caps alone cannot solve structural tensions. A cap that is too low can undermine service quality; one that is too high might preserve revenue at the cost of exclusion. To reconcile this, organisations need adaptive caps—ranges testable against real usage. For instance, mobile-money providers in East Africa, when experimenting with low-value remittance corridors in 2021, tested graduated fee bands against two metrics: the share of transactions completed at the lowest tier and the churn rate of small agents handling cash-in/cash-out. The gradient between these two numbers—user relief and agent sustainability—determined the viable cap.

Shared upside likewise carries a limitation. If the upside feels symbolic rather than material, it can breed cynicism. Some platforms adopt token-based reward schemes that promise future dividends but fail to deliver near-term value. Others over-index on branding—promoting the idea of sharing while retaining an overwhelming share of profits. Alignment must be proportionate to the contributions and risks borne by participants. A cooperative revenue share works when the flows match the story. When misaligned, stories collapse.

The motif of *daylight* returns here. In daylight, revenue is not a secret but a structure. It shapes behaviour upstream: teams design features that are economically sustainable rather than psychologically manipulative. It shapes behaviour downstream: users develop spending habits that reinforce long-term engagement rather than short-term extraction. The more visible the structure, the more predictable the ecosystem becomes.

Transparency also protects organisational memory. Decision logs—pricing updates, threshold rationales, revenue segmentation—create continuity when personnel change. In 2018, several community banking initiatives in the UK's North West adopted "open pricing minutes" that summarised quarterly reviews in plain language. When management cycles turned over, the logs prevented strategic drift and allowed new leadership to iterate on evidence, not instinct. The practice strengthened internal governance and preserved external credibility.

But every model carries unresolved tension. Aligning revenue requires balancing sustainability with accessibility. Fee caps protect consumers but may strain small operators unless offset by volume or subsidy. Shared upside boosts engagement but can complicate accounting and reduce flexibility. Transparent pricing builds trust but invites scrutiny that some organisations may find uncomfortable.

The forward test sits in a single question: can a product grow without shifting costs onto the people who trust it most?

Chapter 10
The Protocol Mindset

The first time a group of strangers tried to rewrite the internet from a community centre in Glasgow, the experiment looked almost embarrassingly small. It was 2017, a wet February evening, and a dozen volunteers had gathered around a folding table with laptops that hummed louder than the radiators. They were not building a cryptocurrency, nor chasing the next speculative boom. They were drafting rules. Not legal codes, not technical specifications, but norms—how to disagree, how to allocate shared funds, how to withdraw gracefully when overcommitted. Only once those lines were settled did they turn to the software that would carry their decisions. Months later, when the project outgrew the room and evolved into a federation of neighbourhood digital services, its founders attributed their resilience to those early conversations in the cold: the code was important, but the rules people could live with were what endured.

That scene captures the quiet provocation at the heart of this chapter: technologies scale only when their social architectures do. It is a claim that unsettles the fashionable fantasy that protocols are neutral, self-governing, and immune to the complexities of human behaviour. In truth, every system carries a grammar—of permission, of participation, of consequence. Some communities name this grammar directly; others bury it beneath jargon, hoping the mechanics will speak for themselves. But the most durable projects, from cooperatives to open-source networks to civic associations, treat rules not as an afterthought but as a form of stewardship. They write them in daylight, update them with humility, and bind them to the very incentives that animate their participants.

What we call the "protocol mindset" is not reserved for developers or policymakers. It is a way of thinking accessible to anyone who has ever asked three deceptively simple questions: Who decides? Who benefits? How is harm handled? These questions appear mundane, yet they have toppled governance models, exposed broken incentives, and illuminated the difference between participation and performance. In recent years, they have become critical as communities experiment with broadened ownership—patronage schemes, point systems, profit-sharing arrangements that let neighbours earn service fees rather than merely consume the product. Ownership becomes a verb, not a noun, when it structures inclusion instead of simply rewarding early insiders.

To understand why this matters now, consider the proliferation of projects that measure without meaning. Dashboards glow with metrics designed to impress investors or partners: monthly actives, gross transaction volume, retention curves that are more artefact than insight. Yet the communities that last—those that trouble the status quo rather than mimic it—measure to learn. They convene monthly user councils not for spectacle but for truth. They ask what is not working, what is confusing, what is unfair. And they alter course accordingly. These learning loops break the longstanding pattern in which the loudest voices shape strategy while the quiet ones adapt or leave. The protocol mindset insists that learning is a structural act, not a stylistic one.

Throughout this chapter, the motif of *the rulebook behind the interface* recurs. It reminds us that every digital experience, every cooperative venture, every collective project is underwritten by procedures and power relations that rarely meet the eye. The healthiest communities expose that rulebook, publish it, and test it. They match grants with codes of conduct. They link rewards to behaviour, not charisma. They design manuals for conflict so disagreements do not metastasise into fractures. And they equip their participants with tools—a one-page due diligence grid, a checklist to audit any project—that turn intuition into inquiry.

But the deeper significance lies beyond any individual technique. The protocol mindset addresses a broader cultural exhaustion with opacity, arbitrariness, and unequal upside. People want institutions, however small, that they can shape rather than simply inherit. They want norms that protect without suffocating, and incentives that amplify contribution rather than speculation. They want structures that do not require saintliness to function. This is why the shift from passive consumption to active participation resonates so strongly: it restores a sense of agency in systems that too often feel immovable.

And yet the tension persists. Rules can empower, but they can also exclude. Shared upside can democratise ownership, but it can also entrench cliques. Learning loops can elevate unheard voices, but they can also slow momentum. The protocol mindset is not a cure-all; it is a discipline. It demands clarity without rigidity, openness without chaos, and accountability without fear.

As we turn towards the practical frameworks in the pages ahead, one question shadows every example and every story: what would it look like to build systems—technical, economic, or communal—that treat participation not as a privilege but as a design principle? The promise of this chapter is not that the reader will find definitive answers, but that they will acquire the habits of inquiry that make better answers possible.

Rules people can live with: Write norms alongside code

In June 2018, the Mozilla Foundation gathered its volunteer maintainers in Berlin for what was meant to be an unremarkable weekend summit. What changed the organisation's trajectory was a single exercise held late on the first evening: every participant was asked to write down one behaviour that had quietly driven them away from previous online communities. The pile filled quickly—interruptions that silenced newcomers, pull-request tantrums, private Slack cliques that made public forums redundant. When the group reconvened the next morning, the facilitators paired each behaviour with a draft norm and asked the maintainers to test them against real scenarios. Within a few hours, they had built the first version of a community code of conduct that, over subsequent months, was bound directly to funding decisions, contributor privileges, and resource allocations. Mozilla released this framework publicly in October 2018. By spring 2019, repeat participation in its civic-tech programmes had risen noticeably, a shift the organisation attributed to quieter voices finally trusting the space enough to return. Five words captured the mood that weekend. *Rules make room for dignity.*

The paradox is stark: why do so many technical communities devote hundreds of hours to code reviews yet treat behavioural norms as optional footnotes? Software engineers will obsess over the difference between a race condition and a memory leak, but rarely confront the social fragilities that destroy projects long before a bug can. The gap persists because norms feel intangible, whereas code feels exact. But norms are not soft power; they are architectural load-bearers. They determine who speaks, who stays, who leaves, who escalates, who hides, and who takes responsibility when a quiet problem becomes a public failure. The refusal to write norms is itself a norm—one that protects incumbents, privileges speed over inclusion, and leaves communities to improvise when conflict inevitably arrives.

Show the mechanism, name it, explain it, and the implications become unmistakable. Consider the Python Software Foundation's adoption of a formal Code of Conduct Committee in 2019, anchored in Portland and composed of volunteers trained in conflict resolution. They did not simply publish a guidelines page; they tied the norms to clear escalation procedures, response timelines, and transparent review logs. The behaviour this produced was visible: contributors moderated their tone on mailing lists, newcomers asked bolder questions, and maintainers addressed disagreements before they calcified. The metric that mattered was not sentiment but participation: the Foundation's annual report noted an increase in first-time contributors to core projects between 2019 and 2021. This is the protocol mindset in practice—rules aligned with the lived reality of the people subject to them.

A second case underscores the point. In April 2020, the OpenStreetMap (OSM) community in the United Kingdom implemented a governance overhaul after several high-profile disagreements about data imports and editorial authority. Instead of drafting broad moral exhortations, OSM UK codified a decision-making charter that combined behavioural norms with operational rules. Disputes over mapping boundaries had to follow a transparent review sequence; contributors who repeatedly ignored the sequence faced temporary edit restrictions. Crucially, grants for local mapping events were tied to adherence to these norms. The outcome was measurable: internal disputes dropped, according to OSM UK's annual meeting minutes, and volunteer retention in regional groups from Manchester to Bristol improved over the following year. Code and norms matured together; neither dominated.

Yet any honest account must acknowledge the counter-example: rules can suffocate. Attempts by large platforms to impose universal behavioural frameworks often produce compliance theatre rather than meaningful change. In 2021, GitHub introduced stricter moderation guidelines that, while well-intentioned, were criticised by maintainers who felt the rules ignored the heterogeneity of their projects. Some communities bristled at what they perceived as external policing, and a fraction of maintainers temporarily migrated their repositories to self-hosted alternatives. The lesson is not that rules fail; it is that rules must be authored by the community they govern. Principles imposed from above fracture trust. Principles shaped from within deepen it.

Reconciling this tension requires precision. People accept constraints when they understand their purpose and can see the behaviour they are meant to shape. A norm such as "respect others" is decorative; a norm such as "disagreements must reference evidence, not personal intuition" is actionable. The visible behaviour attached to the rule makes compliance natural rather than performative. The motif of *rules you can live with* mirrors a domestic truth: households do not survive because someone posts slogans on the fridge; they survive because responsibilities are explicit, predictable, and proportionate.

This clarity matters even more in crypto-adjacent communities, where technical and financial implications amplify social risks. A project that issues grants without specifying behavioural expectations invites misuse. A protocol that delegates governance tokens without defining conflict procedures invites factionalism. A community that claims to be decentralised without naming who mediates disputes is not decentralised; it is unaccountable. Writing norms alongside code is not an indulgence but an insurance policy. It prevents the slow erosion of trust that occurs when decisions appear arbitrary or when harmful conduct is excused because "we need the developer".

The implication for teams building new networks is straightforward: begin norm-writing before code-writing, not after. Ask what behaviours you need to protect the project from collapse. Name the incentives that could pit participants against one another. State clearly how disputes will be addressed. Tie grants, rewards, and privileges to adherence. Make the rulebook small and legible. A project that declares "zero tolerance for harassment" but provides no reporting channel is not safer; it is dishonest. A team that insists "founders decide" without naming when that authority expires creates a monarchy, not a community.

Motifs recur here like quiet anchors: portability, transparency, predictability. A rule people can live with is portable—they can carry it across contexts and know what it demands. It is transparent—its consequences are visible before a breach occurs. And it is predictable—it does not change in the heat of conflict. These qualities determine whether norms support or sabotage a project's ambition. They also reveal a basic design principle: people commit to systems that commit to them.

The question that arcs through all of this—subtle yet insistent—is simple: what constitutes fairness when strangers collaborate? There is no final, universal answer. But there are durable methods. Write norms with the same care as code. Publish them where users can see them before they interact. Review them annually. Test them against the edge cases, not the ideal ones. Treat norms not as moral paperwork but as operational infrastructure. Without them, even the best-engineered systems drift.

Which brings us to the unresolved tension that shadows every project with participatory ambition: how do you craft rules that constrain bad behaviour without constraining initiative? At what point does structure protect, and at what point does it calcify? And who, ultimately, has the legitimacy to revise the norms that everyone must live with? The next pages do not settle these questions; they sharpen them.

Ownership as participation: Broaden upside: patronage, points, and profit-sharing

On a cold morning in February 2019, the residents of Nijmegen in the Netherlands gathered in a modest municipal hall to review the year's accounts for *Wiek-II*, a community-owned wind cooperative founded in 2012. The numbers were unglamorous but transformative: households that had bought a €250 share seven years earlier received modest but steady annual payouts, while the cooperative reinvested surplus income into local energy-efficiency grants. The project had not set out to chase national headlines. Its aim was simpler: share the upside of energy production with the people who lived closest to the turbines. Participation was not a slogan but a financial reality. One villager, a retired teacher, remarked that the attraction was not the money but the feeling that "this turbine works for us". Five words captured the shift. *Ownership shapes behaviour visibly.*

The paradox sits in plain sight: why do systems that claim to be decentralised still centralise the benefits of participation? Blockchain projects invite users to "join the network" yet often treat community labour as disposable until growth stalls. Conversely, centuries-old cooperatives distribute value without the fanfare of token launches. If networks want to endure, they must confront this contradiction directly. Participation that carries no upside is not participation; it is unpaid maintenance. Ownership that exists only as messaging does not broaden agency; it simulates it.

The first claim is simple to show. When people own part of what they use, they behave differently. Mondragón Corporation in the Basque Country—established in 1956 and still one of Europe's largest worker cooperatives—demonstrates this with stark consistency. Worker-owners vote on major decisions, elect their management councils, and receive profit allocations tied to collective performance. The behaviour this produces is measurable: higher internal mobility, lower turnover, and investment choices that favour employment stability over short-term gain. The implication is direct. Ownership is not a perk; it is a governance instrument that influences decisions at every level.

To understand how digital networks can borrow from such models, consider the emergence of local "node economies". In May 2021, the Helium Network piloted neighbourhood-operated hotspots across Lisbon. Individuals who hosted small wireless nodes earned tokens tied to network activity—service fees rather than speculative windfalls. The visible behaviour was striking: hosts monitored coverage gaps, coordinated placement with neighbours, and assisted in troubleshooting because their income depended on network reliability. The network grew through stewardship, not hype. The motif recurs here—*ownership as participation*—a reminder that systems flourish when contribution and compensation move together.

Yet the limitations of this model must be acknowledged. When rewards take the form of tradeable tokens, speculation can distort participation. The 2021–22 wave of play-to-earn projects provides the clearest counter-example. The Philippine user base of *Axie Infinity* initially earned meaningful income, but by early 2022, token prices collapsed. The visible behaviour shifted instantly: users abandoned the game, asset values cratered, and the foundation was forced to revisit its economic assumptions. Participation that relies solely on token appreciation is fragile. It collapses when the financial logic breaks. The lesson is not that tokenised rewards fail; it is that they must be tethered to genuine use, not the promise of indefinite price increase.

Reconciling the promise and peril requires precision in design. Broadened upside works when rewards track the value created, not the volatility traded. Patronage models offer one route. In 2020, *Patreon's* community guidelines revealed a simple truth: creators who shared early drafts, decision notes, and behind-the-scenes materials saw higher retention and more sustained patron support. The behaviour here is visible: meaningful ownership feels like access, context, and contribution, not merely cash. In crypto contexts, community patrons might receive voting credits on specific product directions or early access to usability research. What matters is not the novelty of the reward but its proximity to shaping the project's evolution.

Points systems offer another route, provided they are framed clearly as contribution ledgers, not pseudo-currencies. Wikipedia's long-standing "barnstars"—digital tokens awarded for exceptional contributions since 2003—carry no monetary value yet shape behaviour significantly. Contributors who receive barnstars tend to increase their editing activity in the following weeks, according to internal Wikimedia research (2020). The implication is obvious: recognition is a reward when it emerges from peers, not algorithms. Digital networks can take this logic further by tying points to specific powers: proposal rights, testing privileges, or the ability to trigger review processes.

Profit-sharing models complete the triad. For decades, John Lewis Partnership in the United Kingdom has tied staff bonuses to company performance. While the model has faced pressure in recent years, its cultural impact remains well-documented: staff describe the firm as "ours" rather than "theirs". Translating this to digital networks demands attention to scale. Profit-sharing cannot be an afterthought patched onto a business model optimised for extraction. It must be architected at the start: define what counts as profit, identify who contributed, and allocate rewards proportionately. Payment rails for micro-payouts now make this viable at low cost.

The quiet motif threads through these examples like a seam: *participation must be reciprocal.* A user who reports bugs should see that labour acknowledged. A local host who stabilises coverage should receive a fee, not a thank-you emoji. A community member who mentors newcomers should gain influence, not invisibility. When participation yields no meaningful stake, people retreat. When participation builds a sense of shared upside, people commit.

Now consider the implication for emerging protocols. If ownership is designed as a post-hoc gift, it will be perceived as arbitrary and manipulable. If ownership is designed as a living agreement, it becomes a stabilising force. The distinction is behavioural. In well-designed systems, participants can measure their own stake: they can see how their actions translate into outcomes. When transparency is high and friction is low, the network gains resilience. When rewards are obscure or capricious, participants disengage or attempt to game the system.

A revealing example comes from community mesh networks. Guifi.net, founded in Catalonia in 2004, grew to thousands of nodes by offering contributors clearly defined ownership rights: those who extended the network gained priority bandwidth allocations and decision rights in local governance assemblies. This was ownership made tangible. The network's growth was not fuelled by marketing but by the alignment of incentives with real-world effort. Participants could trace the line from contribution to benefit—a line too many modern networks obscure.

Yet a caution remains. Broadened upside can create hierarchy as easily as it prevents it. Early entrants may accumulate disproportionate influence, turning participatory systems into oligarchies. This is the counter-example worth taking seriously. Token-voting systems have repeatedly fallen into this trap: whales dominate, newcomers disengage, and governance becomes theatre. To reconcile this, designers must commit to one principle: upside must grow with participation, not with mere possession. Sunset clauses for voting power, contribution-weighted reward pools, and caps on influence prevent early concentration from fossilising.

All of this leads to a deeper question that shadows the entire discussion: what does it mean to own part of a protocol? Is ownership a financial stake, a decision right, a reputational asset, or a responsibility? The answer, necessarily, is plural. Ownership is the bundle of consequences that makes participants care enough to act. Remove that, and participation atrophies. Strengthen it, and the network gains the most precious of resources: people willing to steward it when hype fades.

Which leaves the unresolved tension that marks the boundary between clever design and durable community: how broadly can upside be shared before the system becomes too complex to govern? At what point does participation empower, and at what point does it fragment? And who decides when the balance must shift? The next section turns that question outward and asks what systems learn when the community itself becomes the engine of refinement.

Learning loops: Metrics to learn, not to impress

In March 2017, a small civic-tech non-profit in Bristol, *The Restart Project*, realised it had a problem. Attendance at its neighbourhood repair workshops was rising, but the team could not explain why certain events flourished while others remained thinly attended. They had gathered the usual vanity figures—footfall, social-media reach, volunteer hours—but none of these numbers clarified what mattered: which conditions produced durable participation and which quietly undermined it. So they built a monthly user council. Ten residents, each representing a different workshop, met on the first Wednesday of every month to discuss what had actually worked. Within three cycles, a pattern emerged. Events succeeded not because they attracted the most visitors but because hosts greeted every newcomer in the first two minutes. A five-word sentence captured the revelation. *Warm welcomes change everything.* And the organisation rebuilt its playbook around that behaviour.

The paradox remains uncomfortable: why do organisations that claim to be data-driven still cling to metrics that teach them nothing? They celebrate soaring sign-ups but ignore the question that truly tests value—*who came back and why?* They showcase dashboards more intricate than any flight instrument panel yet cannot point to a single decision that changed because of them. Learning loops begin where vanity narratives end. They demand the discipline to measure what is hard, not what is flattering. They ask a simpler, often more moral question: *What do we owe the people who rely on us?*

The first claim requires demonstration. When organisations measure to learn rather than impress, behaviour shifts. The UK's Government Digital Service (GDS), during its 2013–2016 transformation of public websites, published weekly performance dashboards—raw data that exposed where citizens struggled. One page revealed that more than 40% of users attempting to register a Power of Attorney abandoned the process halfway. Naming the pain forced immediate action. The team simplified the flow, reduced the number of screens, and introduced clearer prompts; abandonment fell measurably within eight weeks, a behavioural pivot recorded in transparent logs. The implication was unmistakable. Metrics that embarrass you are the ones that teach you. Metrics that flatter you are the ones that mislead you.

But organisations in the decentralised world have spent a decade constructing the opposite dynamic. They highlight total value locked (TVL) even when it reveals nothing about user well-being. They amplify trading volume even when that volume comes from wash trades. Behaviour follows the incentives. Teams chase the numbers that make their token charts look buoyant because those are the numbers investors demand. Yet none of those metrics answer the most basic governance question: *Is this system genuinely useful to the people we expect to maintain it?* The quiet motif that reappears here—*listen to use, not noise*—is the hinge on which credible systems turn.

A counter-example exposes the danger. In 2022, several decentralised exchanges celebrated their TVL milestones despite unresolved liquidity fragmentation. The visible behaviour was dysfunctional: liquidity providers rotated capital between pools solely to farm short-term incentives, leaving genuine users exposed to price slippage. One exchange publicly admitted the limitation in its January 2023 retrospective, noting that "TVL masked the instability of actual liquidity" and that chasing the metric had become "a distraction from resilience". The reconciliation is blunt but necessary. Any figure that can be gamed will be gamed. Learning loops survive only when they privilege metrics tied to lived experience: session completion, dispute resolution time, user-led improvements, or monthly community reviews.

The example of monthly user councils shows how this principle becomes operational. A user council is not a focus group; it is a governance device. When Transport for London introduced the Dial-a-Ride accessibility user board in 2008, the visible behavioural shift was immediate. Complaints fell not because processes magically improved, but because disabled passengers could now watch their feedback influence scheduling, training, and route planning. The metric that mattered—response time to user-raised issues—became a public commitment rather than an internal afterthought. The implication is structural. When governance allows people to see the effect of their testimony, learning accelerates. When governance hides user voices behind opaque analytics, learning decays.

To borrow from a different domain, consider the shift in clinical audit culture in the NHS following the publication of the *Francis Report* in 2013. Trusts were required to publish "learning summaries" that linked incidents with specific process changes. This created a measurable link between error and learning—a loop rather than a ledger. The behaviour this produced was visible: wards began running "huddle boards" where nurses and clinicians reviewed the previous day's near-misses. The motif echoes again: *listen to use, not noise.* It is a reminder that loops are sustained not by tools but by norms.

Yet even strong learning systems face limitations. Feedback can become performative. User councils can be captured by the most vocal participants. Metrics can harden into new vanity rituals if not interrogated continuously. The counter-example comes from municipal planning. Several European cities expanded participatory budgeting in the mid-2010s, but internal evaluations—such as Lisbon's 2019 review—found that recurring participants dominated submissions while lower-income neighbourhoods remained under-represented. The visible behaviour betrayed an uncomfortable truth: mechanisms designed to democratise learning can entrench asymmetry. Reconciling this requires design that compensates for silence, not just amplifies speech. Weighted sampling, rotating panels, and structured interviews help distribute voice more fairly.

The deeper implication surfaces here. Learning loops are not feedback forms; they are constitutional commitments. They reflect what a project believes about agency. If a network treats people as data points, it measures only what can be tallied. If it treats people as stewards, it seeks signals that demand interpretation. The distinction shows itself during uncertainty. Projects that measure to impress freeze when metrics decline, blaming the user. Projects that measure to learn ask: *What changed in the world that we failed to anticipate?*

Consider the early 2020 usability overhaul of Estonia's *e-Residency* programme. Application numbers had plateaued, and critics argued the scheme was losing relevance. Instead of improving marketing, the team conducted structured interviews across Tallinn and London, revealing that applicants struggled with the identity verification step due to inconsistent embassy hours. The visible metric—verification abandonment—became the anchor for reform. Within six months, Estonia introduced remote video verification with audited security controls. Adoption rose significantly by late 2020. The implication reaches beyond government: learning loops advance only when teams measure the friction users feel, not the prestige metrics they hope to display.

A second example demonstrates how learning loops shape organisational culture. In 2019, the cooperative telecom *The People's Operator UK* ran an internal experiment: each product team committed to publishing a quarterly "learning docket"—three insights gained from failures, tied to specific data points. The behaviour this produced was unexpected. Teams began seeking opportunities to test riskier hypotheses because failure no longer carried stigma; it carried informational currency. The motif threads once more—*listen to use, not noise.* That discipline turns error into guidance rather than embarrassment.

If this seems demanding, it is because true learning costs something. It requires admitting ignorance. It requires treating metrics as questions rather than trophies. But it also yields the one advantage hype-driven projects can never counterfeit: credibility with the people who matter. Credibility is not built through announcements; it is built through accountable iteration.

This introduces the unresolved tension that shadows all learning systems. How do you measure what matters when what matters cannot always be measured—trust in a dispute process, confidence in data handling, the dignity of using a service that does not condescend? Which signals deserve quantification, and which must remain qualitative, contextual, even narrative? And who decides when the balance between rigour and empathy must shift? The next section turns towards that problem, asking how projects can codify norms that people can actually live with, rather than metrics that merely decorate a dashboard.

A playbook for readers: Checklists to audit any project: who decides, who benefits, how harm is handled

In May 2015, the Dutch Safety Board published its review of the municipality of Eindhoven's automated parking-garage system after a software fault caused a full shutdown and stranded hundreds of residents. The failure was not catastrophic, but the report distilled something more revealing than the malfunction itself: no single person could explain who held ultimate authority over code changes, who bore liability for user inconvenience, or who was empowered to halt the system when confusing alarms began. The Board's conclusion was terse. *Critical infrastructure lacked a canonical map of decision and responsibility.* What emerged from the aftermath was striking: a one-page operational grid—roles, triggers, escalation paths—posted in every control room. The grid was not sophisticated. It was simply explicit. And that was enough to restore public confidence.

The paradox persists in many sectors that claim to be cutting-edge. Why can a small municipal department articulate who decides and who benefits, while multimillion-pound technology ventures remain vague about both? Why do organisations capable of writing intricate smart contracts struggle to write a single sheet that explains how harm will be handled? The absence of such maps is not an oversight; it is a risk. Without them, even well-intentioned projects drift towards improvised governance, and improvised governance rarely protects the most vulnerable.

The first claim demands a demonstration. When Václav Havel's Civic Forum in Prague drafted its provisional internal rules in late November 1989—barely days after mass protests—they included a deceptively simple clause: every public statement required dual sign-off by both an elected coordinator and a volunteer representing regional activists. The visible behaviour was unity, not because disagreements disappeared, but because accountability became traceable. The rule was a checklist item: *who approves what, and on whose behalf?* The implication reaches beyond political transitions. Any project that cannot answer that question invites disorder, even if its technology is brilliant.

A quiet motif recurs throughout this subchapter—*maps matter.* They matter because people rely on them when uncertainty strikes. They matter because projects too often confuse ambition with structure. And they matter because trust is rarely granted; it is built through the painstaking clarity of knowing who stands behind a decision.

Consider the first dimension of any audit map: authority. Power obscured is power unchecked. One contemporary example comes from the open-source community. In 2021, the Python Software Foundation (PSF), based in Delaware but with global maintainers, adopted a more formalised steering council protocol after a period of governance strain. The protocol named five elected maintainers, specified term limits, and created an appeal mechanism for community disputes. The visible behaviours were subtle yet decisive: fewer contentious merges, faster resolution of bug triage, and a documented path for volunteers to escalate concerns. The implication is that authority declared publicly becomes authority constrained productively.

The second dimension is benefit. Projects often claim broad public value while distributing actual gains narrowly. A sober example is the rise of *micro-mobility* schemes across European cities in the late 2010s. Operators touted decreased emissions, but city audits—from Paris in 2019 and Copenhagen in 2020—revealed that ridership skewed heavily towards affluent neighbourhoods while the maintenance burden fell disproportionately on underserved districts. The contradiction was empirical. The projects were not harmful by design; they were asymmetric in effect. A due-diligence grid that mapped beneficiaries against burdens would have exposed the imbalance earlier. The motif returns: *maps matter* because they force implicit trade-offs into view.

The third dimension, often the most neglected, concerns harm. Organisations excel at forecasting success but stumble when required to articulate how damage will be recognised, mitigated, and repaired. Here the municipal example of Eindhoven is joined by a second, more sobering case. In 2016, the Australian Census system suffered a widely publicised outage, prompting an investigation by the Australian National Audit Office. The audit found that while technical preparations were extensive, the incident-response plan lacked a clear chain of authority and offered no transparent communication path for the public. The visible behaviour was confusion. Users were told simultaneously to log off and log back on. The implication was severe: harm handling is not crisis improvisation; it is pre-commitment to a process people can follow when stakes rise.

To understand how checklists guide real decisions, notice what they demand teams to reveal. A robust grid asks: *Who decides?* That means naming a role, not a vague committee. *Who benefits?* That means pointing to a quantifiable outcome, not a promise. *How is harm handled?* That means describing the first hour of response, not the press release that comes after. The clarity of these questions is what gives the grid power. It is also what exposes weak governance most quickly.

The strength of this approach becomes evident in projects that adopt it early. In 2018, the cooperative broadband provider *B4RN* (Broadband for the Rural North) in Lancashire published a "community rights and obligations" sheet. It stated, in plain text, how decisions on network expansions were made, who earned from installation contracts, and how service failures would be triaged. The sheet was updated every quarter with annotations explaining what had changed. The behavioural metric was telling: volunteer participation increased by measurable margins in 2019, particularly in areas where roles and rewards had previously been unclear. Maps fostered involvement. The implication is practical. Transparency is not a moral flourish; it is an operational advantage.

A credible counter-example underscores limits. Some blockchain networks began issuing "governance dashboards" around 2020, yet internal reviews—such as Tezos' 2022 community assessment—found that dashboards became decorative. Roles were listed, but authority remained ambiguous. Benefits were proclaimed, but rarely measured against independent evidence. Harm pathways were described, but escalation remained untested. The grids existed, but they were not *maps*—they were brochures. Reconciling this requires embedding due-diligence grids directly into governance, not marketing. A map that is not used to make a decision is not a map at all.

A deeper implication surfaces. Checklists are not reductionist bureaucratic tools; they are cognitive aids that prevent overconfidence. They force teams to confront uncomfortable details. They create a record of intentionality. They reduce the space for retrospective excuses. They allow public scrutiny not because scrutiny is fashionable, but because scrutiny stabilises systems. And they give communities leverage: the ability to point to an explicit commitment and say, *You promised.*

Notice again the motif—*maps matter.* They matter because complexity invites drift. They matter because drift invites harm. They matter because harm denied becomes harm repeated. In this sense, the due-diligence grid is a civic instrument. It is the reader's way into a project's truth. It reveals who has voice, who carries cost, and who receives benefit. It surfaces design choices often presented as inevitabilities. It provides a language of inquiry that any citizen, contributor, or regulator can use.

As this book has argued across preceding chapters, systems endure when accountability is built into the grain of their design. But here the question become sharper. How do we ensure our maps stay accurate as projects evolve? How do we prevent checklists from calcifying into relics? How do we create audit tools that remain alive to shifting power, changing beneficiaries, and emerging harms? The tension is real. And it sets the stage for what follows: how readers can use these tools not just to understand projects, but to interrogate them—fairly, rigorously, and without illusion.

About the Author

Jahan Vespari writes about technology that meets everyday life, with a focus on how design and governance shape who gets served. After years working alongside product teams and civic groups, Vespari has seen that the most durable systems are those people can actually use and trust. Raised on stories of neighbourhood credit circles and mutual aid, Vespari follows a simple thread: finance is a social technology long before it is a digital one. This perspective informs the work here, blending practitioner detail with humane clarity. The mission is straightforward: centre lived problems, treat inclusion as infrastructure, and share playbooks that help readers evaluate claims and build for the long term.

www.ingramcontent.com/pod-product-compliance
Lightning Source LLC
Chambersburg PA
CBHW031344230926
51848CB00002B/377
9789374596425